Allen Lane

Samir Nadim

AC

The Penguin Book of

SQUASH

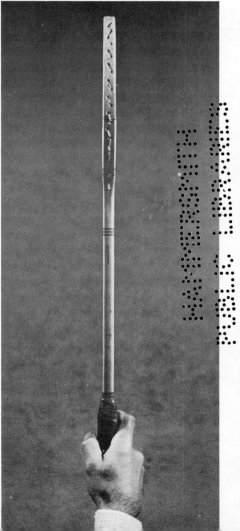

ALLEN LANE
Penguin Books Ltd
17 Grosvenor Gardens
London SW1W 0BD

First published 1979
Published simultaneously by Penguin Books

Copyright © Samir Nadim, 1979

ISBN 0 7139 1166 2

Printed in Great Britain by
E. A. Pindar & Son Ltd, Scarborough, N. Yorkshire

Design by Keith Burns

Set in Monophoto Photina by
Oliver Burridge & Co. Ltd, Crawley

The SRA Rules given in the
Appendix are reproduced with the
kind permission of the Squash
Rackets Association.

*The photographs throughout the book were taken at
St Albans Squash Club.*

Contents

List of plates

List of text figures

Introduction _____

It is regrettable that most enthusiasts, although they certainly enjoy themselves, never bother to learn to play squash correctly. Their approach overlooks one very important and fundamental key that, if applied, would always ensure a more satisfying and rewarding game. That key is *the attitude of mind of the player towards the game.* To become a consistently efficient player, you must get into harmony with a definite law, one which has many ramifications, and which will alter your whole approach and mental attitude towards the game. The aspects of this law, as they apply to squash, are revealed in this book. To understand the law you must experience it while playing. When applied it inevitably brings good results; if ignored or opposed it leads to poor sportsmanship, dangerous play, and general frustration.

I would like to tell you the story behind this book, as it has a strong bearing on my attitude to squash as it is played today, at all levels.

In my many years of professional coaching I have discovered that the greater part of the game is shrouded in a fog of mystery. It seemed that anyone could learn to play the game, by watching others, by getting a friend to introduce them to the game, by going on a court alone and knocking the ball up and down, by hiring a coach to show them how to hold the racket, teach them the rules and tactics, or even by purchasing one of the many books that are available. But it seemed that no one could discover, or was able to pass on to others, concrete evidence that they either knew or understood the fundamentals and principles behind the game. In other words, the cause-and-effect relationship was totally unknown, even in the upper echelons of players and coaches. I came to England to represent Egypt in the 1960 World Championships at the Royal Automobile Club. As I had achieved a place as an international, playing for the top team in the world at that time, I was aware that I was a good player, but only up to a point. I was at this time unable to see my own faults, or to understand the reason for my occasional failures. I decided to consult a top coach who was resident in England at that time, and ask him if he could help me.

During my lesson, I told the coach that when I practised hitting the ball down the side wall, fast and low, I sometimes hit the tin, or the ball would glance off the side wall and divert from the straight. I asked him to tell me where I was going wrong, and how to correct it. His answer was that I needed to practise more. Of course, I told him that I practised for many hours every day, and he went on to say that he meant that I should practise that particular shot until I could do it ten times out of ten. A lot of people would have given up here, but I was determined to have my question answered, and ploughed on. I told him that although I frequently could perform this exercise, there were times when I couldn't. I seemed to fail just when I needed to succeed most, namely, when playing a match which depended on my gaining that particular point. I explained that I felt let down and frustrated, not only because I had lost the match, but also because I did not know why! Obviously I must be doing something wrong, surely he could see that? Still no satisfactory answer was forthcoming. I finally gave up, coming to the conclusion that we were each as ignorant as the other.

When I turned professional, I had no teaching experience; all I could do was give my pupils a good game, help them to enjoy it, improve their fitness, sharpen them up, etc. So, being very new to coaching, I approached a number of experienced coaches and asked for their assistance and advice, only to discover, yet again, that none of them was able to give me any *constructive* advice. At that time I felt strongly that they simply did not want to share their expertise with me, a newcomer, but I now realize that they did not have anything to offer, anything that they *could* share with me. Obviously I was alone in trying to pierce the fog, or, indeed, in believing that it existed. I must stress that the people who were at the top of the game at that time genuinely felt that they had the answer, and were doing their very best to teach those people who looked to them for help. Their knowledge was partial, however; some of the things they were teaching were actually contradictory. They were dealing with the effects, but failing to penetrate to the causes. Nevertheless they were sincere, serving the game to the best of their ability.

It was at this time, and because of these experiences, that I decided that I was going to explore the facts behind the game, the cause and effect. After all, most of the components are consistent, the walls, the ball and the racket remain the same, the human body follows the same pattern, so why are the results not equally consistent? The answer must lie in the only unpredictable factor, the player's mind.

It therefore seemed that if I could make the player aware of the laws which applied, and encourage him to use the correct actions at all times, surely the results would be phenomenal! All that remained was for me to discover these laws, and the principles behind them: how far the ball travelled between bounces, where the best striking point was, at what angle the face of the racket should meet the ball, which part of the arm delivered the most power and control, and so on.

I began my research. I travelled everywhere, constantly learning, probing and analysing, thinking and improving. In the first four years, up to 1966, I learned a lot, gathering information on the variability of the human factor and on the questions which were worrying players of different standards. It was at this time that I decided to write a book — a book which would collate all the experience that I had gained.

Obviously this needed a totally different approach. More consideration and deeper thought had to be given to the project. My involvement at this time with Ambassador College gave me the self-knowledge and inner strength required to approach the task. After a further seven years of experimenting I began to write the book in 1973, and it took a further four years to get the results of these experiments, and my thoughts, down on paper. Although able to speak English quite fluently, I do not find it easy to express myself on paper, and I received a great deal of assistance from my English friends.

This is probably the best time for me to thank those who helped me to complete this book — people who had faith in me and my methods, like Eddie Smith, who (although he had never played any type of sport and was therefore at a great disadvantage), with his humility and understanding, set me a fine example. Also a former squash pupil, Sandy Adamson who, upon joining my organization, discovered the manuscript tucked away in a drawer where it had been relegated, polished it, and gave me no peace until it had been accepted by the publishers. Without these people, and the many others who have given me help and encouragement, my dream of making successful squash available to everyone, young or old, would still be but a dream.

Seven years later, and the book is complete. All my field tests have been carried out and proved, and the several hundred guinea pigs are well on the way to successful squash. I now pass the message on to you in this book. Of course you must realize that all the mystery of the game will be lost! When you discover for yourself that one and one makes two, that all you have to do is follow the rules to make your game consistent, and when you know exactly why the ball behaves as it does, there will be no more surprises and no more frustration . . . How boring the game will become! Or will it?

So, will you join me in my revolution? Help me to make squash the most rewarding and skilful game in the world today. Help me to prove that there is no 'typical squash player'. Dispel the myth of a select group of people who bear charmed rackets, and who own hidden secrets. Anyone with two arms and two legs can play, and play well; all it takes is a little dedication. No inborn skill is required, although of course it will always come in very handy. I have already proved that a man who has the use of only one eye can play at competitive club standard after only four months' coaching, so those who are fortunate in having all their faculties need have no qualms about taking up the game. Neither is age a barrier, although a gradual approach is recommended for the older player if he has not had a sporting background, or if he is extremely unfit. But with care, and with the help of an understanding coach, you will find, not only that the game is still very enjoyable when played at a slightly more gentle pace, but also that the exercise will help your body to function more efficiently because of the improved blood flow. Don't forget – no one can become a veteran squash champion under the age of forty-five!

True, many of those who *have* become interested in squash have thought to themselves, or, in some cases, have said frankly to me, 'Why do I need lessons? I don't aspire to be a champion, I only want to play for the enjoyment and exercise.' There may be many reasons why a person would not wish to commit himself to coaching; nevertheless a course of lessons, or this book, or, better still, the two combined, would be an invaluable base from which to proceed.

One of the most important, and easily forgotten, points is that, without coaching, players may tend to swing wildly at the ball, so risking striking each other with their rackets. (According to the latest figures, the number of injuries reported has reached mammoth proportions.) Is it not more courteous to show concern for your fellows by learning to play correctly from the beginning, thereby eliminating the risk of injuring another person?

In writing this book I hope to pass on to you, the reader, a greater enthusiasm and love for squash than you have hitherto experienced. I shall also have something to say about that dimension which I feel is missing from squash today. I hope that it will give you – as it has me – a new sense of achievement in your game.

1· Taking up squash

This is a transcript of a conversation between myself and a prospective pupil, someone who had decided to take up the game later in life than most.

Pupil: Mr Nadim, I have played a little squash and enjoyed it. I would like to be good, and I wondered if you taught people like me, or only sporty types?

Samir: Right. Now sit down, and we'll have a talk, because this is something that I feel really strongly about. When a person comes to me asking to learn, and begins by qualifying himself, saying things like 'I'm not a sporty type' or 'I know I could never be a good player', or 'But I can't do that!', he is already beaten.

Pupil: But perhaps they genuinely feel that because they have never been sports-minded, or because their bodies aren't built athletically, or maybe because they think that they're too old, they shouldn't presume to ask you?

Samir: Oh they use those excuses, and many more, anything they can think of. They are totally negative. What I say to them is this, No matter who you are, all you have to do is obey the laws which I will teach you, learn to identify with them, work with them, put them into practice. Appreciate the need to hold on to them in your squash life and the end result will be success and nothing but success.

Try to look at it this way. When you go to university, there are a lot of years of learning ahead of you, but you know that at the end of them you will get a degree. Some pass with honours because they are more capable, others just pass, but they are still good — they have got a degree. It's the same in squash, you study, apply yourself, and you pass. You're good, you've a very good standard. But, if you can't be bothered, if you want to belong to the nobodies, then by all means continue to be negative. Alternatively, if you want to be somebody, forge ahead. It might take you longer than another person. So what! That person is *more* capable, and can achieve more. Maybe more will be expected of him once he has obtained his degree — the standard which you, and everybody else, can reach. That you *can* reach it I have proved, not once, but many times over.

Pupil: So are you honestly saying that you could bring someone like me, who has never participated in any ball game, is overweight, and probably too old for the game anyway, up to that standard?

Samir: The answer is yes, if you're willing to go through with it, whatever it takes.

Pupil: Must I make a mental adjustment then — believe that I can do it?

Samir: It is a mental attitude in that you must put your mind to it.

Pupil: It seems to me that you're offering me the blueprint, and it's up to me to go out and build a squash player.

Samir: Sure, you can do it. In the beginning you will need help and reassurance, because confidence only comes as you go along, after you have seen the results, and learnt to prove all the things that I say. There will come a time when you will realize that it's not just Samir's ideas and suggestions, but that they work anyway, with or without me. I can only tell you that these rules exist; it's up to you to prove it, because proving it is a vital ingredient. An inner conviction is necessary; the result is always an absolute. Once you have come into contact with it, and have begun to use it yourself, seeing, and believing in what you see, then you will begin to have confidence, and begin to believe in *yourself*. You will overcome that weakness which makes you say 'I can't'. This is one of the negative signs which some people use as a barrier against trying, because they are afraid they will fail.

Pupil: What about fitness?

Samir: If you want to be fit, we can make you fit.

Pupil: No, sorry, what I meant was, do I have to make the effort to get fit in order to play squash, or will squash in itself make me fit?

Samir: Well, I have to qualify that. If a person was very fat or unfit, it would be irresponsible to ask too much of him on court. Obviously we would have to consider many things: his heart, his breathing, his blood flow and his diet. Do whatever it takes, which is what I said earlier. If you're willing to go through with it, we can make it. I've done it before, that's why I know. Not think, *know*. And I will do it again, any time, regardless of who it is.

Pupil: Regardless? Do you never fail?

Samir: No. We have never had a failure, and we never will.

Pupil: That's good enough. I'm willing if you are. Where do we start?

Sandy Adamson writes:
I can attest to the fact that this was an actual conversation because I was the prospective pupil. At first I found the thought of the effort involved quite daunting, but gradually I came to realize that all Samir had said was true, that the biggest battle I had to fight was a mental one. (I am still fighting it to some degree.) Even so, I have the deep conviction that the way I am learning is the right way, because I have proved it for myself. I no longer have to be told what I have done wrong, as I know immediately I have done it. I suppose it is rather like those occasions when your car breaks down. You lift the bonnet and stare helplessly at the engine,

hoping that whatever is broken will be obvious to you — a vain hope to those not acquainted with the secrets of the internal combustion engine. A mechanic has all the mysteries revealed to him, and can confidently diagnose the trouble. This is the way I now feel about squash. I may not be at the required standard yet — that is my body's fault — but I know the reason for everything that happens on court, and I know what I must do to attain the much desired success. When you know what you must do it is comparatively easy to achieve, easier than trial and error, which is time-consuming and frustrating. One feels totally confident that, with time, one can fit that blueprint of a good squash player.

2 · First things

A DESCRIPTION OF THE COURT

The dimensions of all courts are standard, the playing area being 32 ft long by 21 ft wide. (See figures 1, 2 and 3.) The lower cut line on the front wall is 6 ft above the floor. The upper out-of-court line is 15 ft from the floor at the front, descending to 7 ft from the floor at the back. The short line is 18 ft from the front wall, and the service boxes are 5 ft.3 ins square. The half court line runs from the middle of the short line to the back wall of the court.

The walls are white or near-white in colour. All lines and markings are 2 ins wide, and painted red. Across the front wall there is a 'board' or 2-inch strip of wood, again painted red. Below this is 'the tin' or metal strip which is 19 ins high, and is sometimes called the 'till' or 'tell-tale'. Any ball striking this resonant material is regarded as out of court.

The front facing wall of the court must be solid while the side and back walls can be of wood or composition. Many modern courts feature a back wall made of glass. A court may have glass panels in the roof for daylight play. There will also be at least six electric lights, or fluorescent strips, suspended above the court to ensure proper lighting. For those courts situated below ground, artificial lighting is the only possible method. Proper ventilation and heating systems are necessary to cope with differing temperatures, changes of weather, and the condensation brought about by large numbers of spectators.

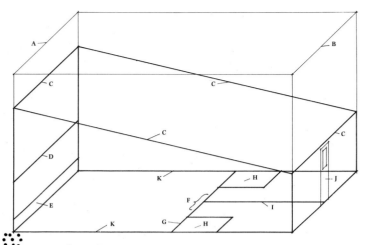

Figure 1. Three-dimensional view of a squash court.

Our drawings show the markings and layout of a singles court. Explanations are given below.

A. The Front Wall: the focal point of the court. Any shot played *must*, at some time, touch this wall before bouncing on the floor, or being returned by an opponent.

B. The Back Wall: generally of solid composition up to balcony level, allowing a restricted number of people to watch the game. Some courts have glass backs, permitting a large number of spectators, and lending themselves admirably to group coaching.

C. The Out-of-Court Line: this red line stretches all round the court, descending from 15 ft high at the front wall, to 7 ft high at the back. Any ball going over, or touching, this line is out of play.

D. The Cut Line: only used for service. The server must play the ball so that it hits the front wall between this and the upper out-of-court line and touching neither.

E. The Tin: can be found below the lower out-of-court line on the front wall. Any ball hitting the tin is out of play.

F. The T: once a rally is in progress, players should aim to be standing in the general area of the T. Any player in this position can generally dominate the game, as he is then standing at the shortest distance from any part of the court. He can easily retrieve his partner's shot and place his own at the furthest distance from his partner. (See 'False Concepts: The T Area', p. 127).

G. The Short Line: once again this is only used for service. On its return from the front wall, the ball must land behind the short line and within the opposite quarter of the court.

H. The Service Box: whether the server is serving from the forehand or backhand court, he must have at least one foot in the box, not touching any of the lines, at the moment that his racket strikes the ball.

I. The Half Court Line: for service only. This line divides the court into the forehand and backhand courts and designates the back quarter of the court within which the served ball must land.

J. The Door: no explanation necessary. To open the door of a court without first checking whether that court is in use is extremely dangerous!

K. The Nick: junction of any wall and the floor. Although this is not an official marking or position, it is worth a mention as it will doubtless rear its head at some time during play. Any ball landing on this precise point will behave erratically, which can be an advantage or a disadvantage, depending on whether you or your opponent played the shot. Some top players practise to hit this point in order to catch their partner off balance, but it takes considerable skill and know-how to be able to do it consistently. As the ball has hit the side wall and the floor simultaneously, it is considered to have bounced

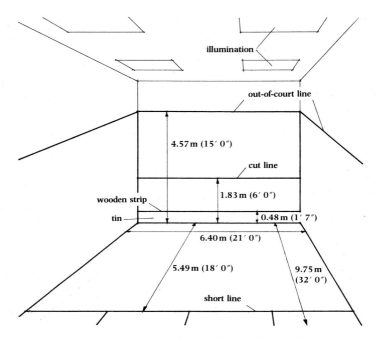

illumination

out-of-court line

4.57 m (15′ 0″)

cut line

wooden strip

1.83 m (6′ 0″)

tin

0.48 m (1′ 7″)

6.40 m (21′ 0″)

5.49 m (18′ 0″)

9.75 m (32′ 0″)

short line

Figure 2. Looking towards the front wall.

once, and must be played before bouncing again. (The rules state that each player is allowed one bounce per stroke.) If the ball rolls along the floor after hitting the nick, it will be impossible to play and is classed as a double bounce.

APPROPRIATE CLOTHING

The rules of the game state simply that 'Players are required to wear white clothing. The referee's decision thereon will be binding.'

The basis for this rule is that white clothing against a white wall will be less distracting for your partner. Squash is a fast and hot game, and the correct dress is the best dress.

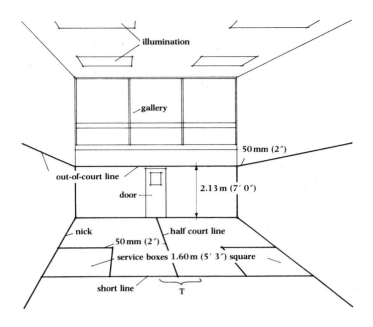

Figure 3. Looking towards the back wall.

The most usual dress for men is white shorts, a white short-sleeved shirt (of the tee-shirt type), and white canvas shoes. The soles of the shoes must not be black, otherwise the court floor will very quickly become scarred and marked.

For women, the dress can vary but usually consists of either a white blouse or shirt with a skirt or shorts, or a white dress.

As regards the current trend towards coloured clothing, any light or pastel shades are acceptable, but my preference will always be for white clothing, as the eye could be a bit slow, and the colours could deceive you, distracting the eye from the ball. It has never been proved, but it is possible that a player wearing garish colours – a boldly striped jumper, for instance – could totally destroy his partner's concentration. But if a snappy outfit makes you feel more confident, then by

First things 25

all means wear it, as long as your partner has no objections. Please be courteous and remember that, in any sort of competition, the umpire will have the final say regarding a dispute over dress. The SRA consider shoes to be a part of your clothing, so the same rules apply — no bright red shoes!

Choosing the right shoes is something that no one can do for you as only *you* know which ones are the most comfortable, but a few guidelines may be helpful. Some people feel that a lighter shoe means less work for the legs, but serious bruising can result from wearing a shoe which does not have a thick enough sole, so a balance must be drawn between a light shoe and one which harms your feet. Footwear is most important — the old horseman's adage, 'No foot, no horse', applies equally to squash. Blisters and bruising can keep you out of the game for weeks.

The best shoes I ever wore were a pair designed for basketball by an American firm. I never had any bruising, hard skin, blisters or pinching, but they were top-quality shoes and extremely expensive. For general use I recommend Dunlop Silver or Green Flash shoes, or something similar; they are high-quality shoes and sell at a reasonably low price. Of course there are more expensive shoes on the market. You may decide after playing for a time that your feet are sensitive and require luxury treatment, but check first that the blisters appearing on the tops of your toes are not due to loose shoes rather than wrong ones. Wearing two pairs of squash socks usually ends this problem. Bruised heels may be the result of too much foot stamping — try to be lighter on your feet.

Another point to consider is that some court surfaces are different from others, and certain makes of shoe may slip on them. Test your shoes first, or ask other club members for their advice on the gripping qualities of the shoes they favour.

THE SQUASH RACKET

The SRA Rules state that the framework of the head of the racket must be made of wood, whereas the handle can be of wood, cane, metal or glass fibre. Gut, nylon or synthetic stringing may be used. A new type of racket with a metal head has recently been developed, but as the SRA and other interested bodies are still deciding whether it is safe to use it is being discouraged at club level. As I personally have never used one, I am unable to comment on its performance. It does not break easily, but it can split, and it also tends to bend if you hit the wall.

The racket grip can be made of any suitable material, i.e. rubber, towelling, or leather. This is very much a matter of personal choice, and you will quickly find which suits you best.

The racket must not exceed twenty-seven inches in length, but no weight limits are specified. They are made to suit most people, some with light heads, others with heavy ones. Some are balanced in the middle. Rackets are supplied with long, short, large or small grips to suit the size of hand. To establish the thickness of the grip, one should make sure that when gripping the racket the third finger is *almost* touching the base of the thumb. If the finger overlaps this point, the grip is too small.

If you are a beginner, you probably do not yet know what weight or balance you require. This is a time when a coach or other experienced player can help you. Perhaps you are fortunate and have a resident coach at your club who also handles sports equipment. Ask him for his help. If he knows your game at all, he will be able to suggest the type of racket you need. Otherwise, pick a good sports shop in your area, and spend some time choosing a racket which 'feels' right. Not too heavy, but comfortable and strong.

Prices vary somewhat, but as a general rule I don't advise people to buy a cheap racket to start with, moving on to a more expensive one later when they improve. This is so often a false economy, as the cheap ones tend to break more easily —

besides, when you're a beginner you need all the help you can get. A good racket feels right and helps your confidence. My colleagues and I personally favour the Dunlop Maxply Fort as it has strength and balance, but there are many equally good rackets on the market, and, as I said earlier, time should be spent on choosing the right one. If you follow the rules, keeping the correct distance from the walls and using the wrist, there is less likelihood of breaking your racket on the walls of the court. Another bonus I can offer you!

People often ask me what type of stringing I use in my rackets, gut or synthetic, as they would like the same in theirs. I tell them that professional squash players are rather like racing drivers in that we need the equivalent of a formula one car for our job. Therefore we use highly expensive gut in our rackets, which are the tools of our trade. A beginner probably will not need this high quality for some time. The synthetic strings are nearly, but not quite, as good as gut. The difference between the two is simply that one is alive, and the other is dead.

Try them both at the beginning of your squash career, and you will not feel a great difference. But if you begin with synthetic and later on change to gut, you will then have the experience to appreciate that it has a lively response, and imparts power as synthetic cannot. Using synthetic strings, you lose pace and touch.

So why not always use gut?

(a) When used in damp conditions, the tension tends to go, so, in this situation, one should use synthetic strings, which are stable.

(b) Gut wears more quickly, and is extremely expensive if you use high quality material.

Even so, a good player will always use gut where possible.

As regards tension, every individual must discover for himself what tension he prefers. If you are a top player, you should aim to have your racket strung at a slightly higher tension than you require, as, within a very short time, the racket will settle into your ideal tension. If you only play occasionally, without much power, then your strings will

remain at the original tension for much longer. (The tension
is measured by poundage.)

THE BALL

Squash balls must be of the type specifically approved for
championship play by the International Squash Rackets
Federation. If they have passed the testing committee
specifications, then they will bear the standard SRA mark.

The ball is small, just over one and a half inches (about
4 cm) in diameter. It is composed of rubber, and comes in
black, green or blue, depending on the manufacturer. It has
an even matt surface.

You will find that most clubs do not allow black balls to be
used, as they mark the white walls and cleaning is expensive.
They are used in championship play only, so choose one of
the 'non-marking' balls which are available in all sports
shops.

The balls are graded as follows:

Yellow Dot	*Extra super slow*	For use on hot courts and in hot countries.
White Dot	*Slow*	For use on cold courts.
Red Dot Blue Dot	*Medium* } *Fast*	Both for use on freezing cold courts, or by beginners. (See 'False Concepts' p. 126, for explanation.)

3 · Getting started

Recall all that you have learned about the court. Notice as
you stand in it the positions of the front wall, the back wall,
the two side walls, the out-of-court lines marked on the walls,
and the tin. Study the plans of the court again. Remember, the

Figure 4. The ball is allowed to bounce on the floor once only
before being returned.

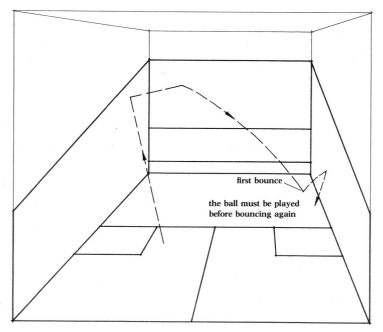

first bounce

the ball must be played
before bouncing again

ball must not touch the out-of-court line, nor the wall above it. It can sail high into the air, but must not hit the ceiling. Therefore, the area of play is below the out-of-court line and above the tin.

The idea of the game is for the two players to hit the ball alternately, the ball always hitting the front wall before being struck by the other player, and always staying within the boundary lines.

It may go directly to the front wall;
or go via a side wall to the front wall;
or go from the back wall, ultimately hitting the front wall;
or it may hit as many walls as possible, providing that the front wall was one of them, *in no particular order!*

Another rule to learn: before being returned, the ball may bounce on the floor once, or not at all, as in the volley (figure 4). If the ball goes to the side wall, then to the front wall, bounces off the floor, and then hits a side wall, we should not let it bounce again on the floor before striking it, because it would then have bounced twice. So, only hit the ball once, and only let it bounce on the floor once, irrespective of the configuration of play.

SCORING

The method of scoring used in squash is clearly laid out in the SRA rules, which are printed in the appendix of this book, but I have included here a simplified explanation to assist beginners.

The game consists of two players, each trying to score nine points before his opponent. Whichever player scores the nine points first wins the game. In the case of a tie at eight points all, refer to the SRA Rules, p. 165. The match will be won by the player who wins the best out of five games.

Squash differs slightly from games like tennis in that you can only score when you have served (at which time you are designated 'hand in') and have subsequently won that rally. When receiving service you are called 'hand out', and you will be unable to score until you have won a rally, and so regained service.

The right to serve first is usually decided by a spin of the racket, caller asking for 'rough' or 'smooth'. (The brightly coloured thin nylon cord on the racket has a rough and smooth weave, and whichever comes uppermost wins the call.) Thereafter, 'hand in' continues to serve until he loses a rally. His partner then becomes 'hand in', and so on, throughout the match.

TO SERVE

1. You must have at least one foot in the service box, and it must not be touching any of the boundary lines at the moment the ball hits the racket.

2. You must hit the ball (without bouncing it on the floor) directly to the front wall, ensuring that impact is above the cut line, and below the upper out-of-court line, and touches neither.

3. Upon its return from the front wall, the ball must fall within the back quarter of the court opposite to that in which the server is standing. The relevant areas are shaded in figure 5.

WHERE TO STAND WHEN RECEIVING SERVICE

Since the ball must fall within the area shown in figure 5, it is best to take up a central position, halfway between the half court line and the side wall, approximately two feet (60 cm) behind the service box (as in figure 5). This position will allow you room to play your shot regardless of where your partner's service lands. Please do not watch the front wall while waiting for service, watch your partner. You can then anticipate the type of service he plans to make and prepare yourself accordingly.

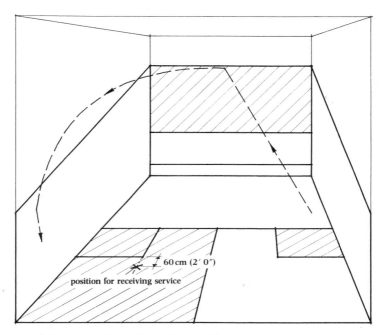

60 cm (2′ 0″)

position for receiving service

Figure 5. Serving from the right-hand box with the relevant areas shaded.

I have gone into the actual methods of serving and receiving in chapters 8 and 9. The most important thing to learn at this stage is how to hit the ball properly. We can then consider the rules of the game in more detail.

4 · The grip, the wrist and how the racket strikes the ball ___

THE GRIP

The correct grip is illustrated in the photographs that follow. You will find that it works equally well for right- or left-handed players.

Grip the racket firmly, but not too tightly, forming a V shape with the thumb and forefinger aligned along the shaft (plates 1–3). There should be a gap between the forefinger and middle finger (plates 1 and 3a).

This grip will not feel natural at first; most people would rather hold the racket in a way that *feels* natural but is in fact naturally wrong (plate 4). How can I maintain that one way is better than another? Well, to begin with, we need one grip, and one grip only, that will eliminate confusion and replace it with success. And, taking all the facts of the game into consideration, *this* is the grip. It never changes, and can be used to play the ball on any part of the court, something which the naturally wrong grip cannot do. It does take getting used to, but it will always keep the racket straight and correctly aligned.

It must be obvious that by using one grip consistently, the player avoids the confusion which would arise from changing his grip for different shots. If he just uses the one grip, as illustrated, and uses it all the time, he need learn no other.

It will take perseverance, and character, to make this grip second nature to you. Resist all desire to revert to what feels most comfortable, and, in time, this correct and very effective

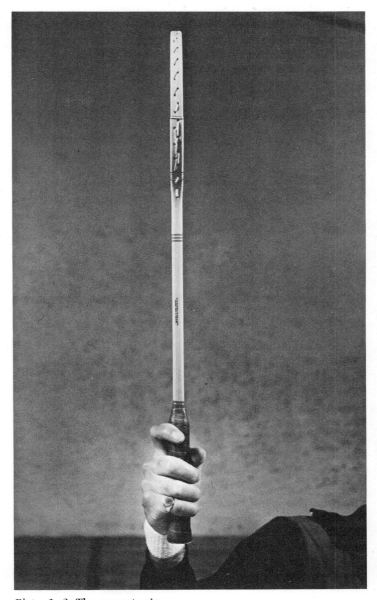

Plates 1–3. **The correct grip.**
Plate 1. The racket is straight in the grip and there is a gap between the forefinger and the middle finger.

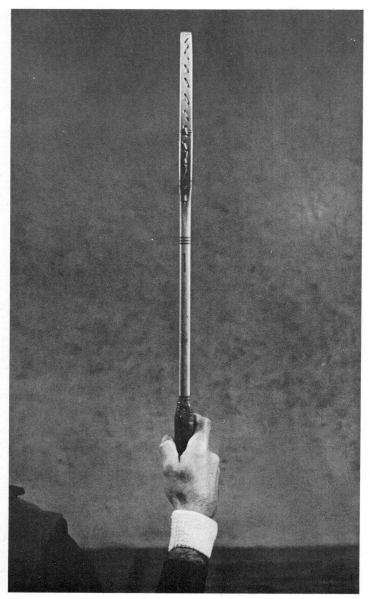

Plate 2. Notice the 'V' and the straight racket as an extension of the arm.

Plates 3a and b. The correct grip in actual play. The same grip is used for forehand and backhand.

Plates 4a and b. The incorrect grip. Notice how ugly and uncomfortable it looks! In both pictures the racket is twisted.

grip will become normal to you. It is possibly the most difficult battle you will have, but when you begin to see the results, you will know that it has been well worth the effort. There are also other reasons for using the correct grip, and these will be mentioned later.

THE WRIST

Here are some of the reasons why one should use the wrist and not the arm when making a stroke:

(a) If you use the full length of your arm when striking the ball, you could find yourself becoming a danger to your opponent. Your play could become *very* dangerous if, when making a powerful stroke, you were unable to stop your arm following through. If, however, you use your wrist to determine the strength of your shot, you will release the impact at the time of striking the ball and you will find that the threat of hitting your opponent with your racket when following through is greatly diminished.

IMPORTANT NOTE. Although it is the opponent's responsibility to stay clear of you when you are striking the ball, that does not give you the right to hit him with your racket. Ask for a 'let' instead, always. (See chapter 14.)

(b) When playing close to a wall, whether it be front, side, or back, if it is your habit to use your arm rather than your wrist to play the shot, you will end up by breaking your racket — ultimately many rackets — on the wall. If, on the other hand, you have anticipated the danger, you may shy away, trying to avoid striking the wall and damaging your racket. Here again, the shot will be unsuccessful.

(c) By playing with your arm instead of your wrist, you will soon tire — you will use up too much energy — whereas using the wrist takes little effort and preserves stamina.

(d) Hitting out at the ball with the full length of your arm limits the effectiveness of touch: you will have no finesse. Using the wrist will ensure that the ball always *zips* away from your racket and flies off the wall because of the *whiplash*

Plates 5 and 6. Correct racket height, forehand and backhand: notice how the head of the racket is just above the wrist. The grip axis of the racket is thus parallel to the floor.

action that the wrist produces. When cracking a whip, you must flex the arm in such a way as to cause the *wrist* to make it crack – try to develop that same action in squash.

(e) You will be late in preparing for the next stroke because of time needed to recover from the mental and physical effort put into the stroke.

Get the best out of your wrist by gripping the racket firmly, but not tightly.

Always hold your racket as though you were holding a small bird. If you hold it too loosely it will fly away, if too tightly you will kill it. If you hold your racket with just the right amount of grip, you will not lose that grip.

I wish to re-emphasize the point that if you use your wrist you will always have more control over the ball and, also, an increased rhythm of play. The ball will travel faster, and with far less effort.

Yet another reason for advocating the grip illustrated is that, if the wrist is correctly and gently used, right from the beginning, you will find that the muscles of your wrist and forearm will work effectively without pain or soreness, and without causing painful after-effects such as tennis elbow.

Pupil: How much should I cock my wrist?

Samir: I can best illustrate this point by telling you a story. It's true, and may interest you.

I was coaching a person recently who had read one of the many books on squash. I won't say which one. He told me, after I had repeatedly asked him to use more wrist, that the book told him that he should cock his wrist, and that he had modelled himself exactly on the picture in the book. Unfortunately, either it hadn't been made very clear, or he had misunderstood, because the poor man wasn't aware that his wrist should also move backwards and forwards, remaining fluid. He was keeping his wrist rigidly cocked and his arm stiff. Consequently, in order to hit the ball, he was forced to move his whole upper body. You can imagine how difficult it was for him. I felt so sorry for him. It took me over ten lessons to help him to adjust psychologically.

Cocking your wrist simply means that you should always keep the head of the racket just above the level of your wrist, keeping that joint fluid. (Figure 6 and plates 5, 6 and 7.)

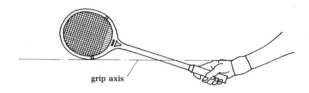

grip axis

Figure 6. The cocked wrist

(i) the head of the racket is just above the wrist;
(ii) the axis is parallel to the floor.

Pupil: I am always being told to keep my racket up, is this what is meant?

Samir: It is a human tendency to leave the racket trailing between shots and, to counteract this, coaches tell you to keep the racket up. The level at which you're told to hold it depends on the coach. Some will tell you to hold it at head height, some chest height, shoulder height, or eye level. Some will even tell you to hold it above your head. All of these are wrong.

In your case, you have a tendency to leave your racket trailing between strokes. Obviously, if your racket is just dangling from your hand you lose valuable time (plate 8). Your stroke preparation takes that bit longer because you have to lift your racket before you can line it up with the ball. If you keep it always at the correct height, that at which the ball is travelling, you will always be ready waiting for the ball (plate 7). You will also run less risk of tangling it between your own, or your partner's, legs!

The grip, the wrist and how the racket strikes the ball 43

A. Notice how the wrist is bent backwards and is still cocked in the right position. This provides power.
B. Notice the bent arm and the way the arm is positioned. The combination of these two will give a fluid wrist and a whiplash action.

Plate 7. Ready and waiting for the ball — fluid wrist.

Plate 8. Trailing racket.

Pupil: So there are two distinct points here. One is the amount your wrist should be cocked, and the other is the linkage between the waiting racket and the height of the ball? (Plates 9, 10 and 11.)

Samir: Yes, try to remember them both, they are both vital. My criticism of you at the moment is that when you play a low shot, you have a trailing racket and a limp wrist. But when playing a volley you automatically cock your wrist, as you cannot play this shot with your racket hanging down. This must help you to prove the theory for yourself. I realize that there are a lot of things to remember when meeting the ball, but try to train yourself to hold the racket at the required height (plates 9, 10, 11), even if it means walking around the house holding your racket for a set time every day. This sounds outlandish, but it is excellent training, and it helps your grip too.

THE OPEN FACE

To ensure that the ball always hits the wall above the tin, move the forearm and wrist, and hit the ball with an open-faced racket.

Remember that the correct grip is not the only thing which dictates an open face; your lower arm must help by twisting gently, until the required angle is achieved and presented to the ball.

Do not try to hit the ball hard at first. Just use your wrist and forearm together gently, until your mind and your muscles begin to work in harmony. Later on, when they know what is expected of them and you have acquired the knack, you can begin to incorporate more force and snap your wrist harder.

In order to hit the ball correctly, the racket must be held on an open-faced plane, and must be brought through level with the height of the ball. See figure 7 and plates 12–15,

Plates 9, 10 and 11. Relationship between waiting racket and height of the ball. Wherever the ball is, the racket is ready and waiting and linked with the flight path of the ball.

Plate 10

Plate 11

Plate 12. The straight racket.
You must be sure that the racket is
absolutely straight as you grip it.

Plate 13. The racket fractionally open
to hit just above the tin.

Plate 14. The open-faced racket. For hitting a higher ball.

Plate 15. The closed racket. There is a
danger of hitting the tin or the floor.

which show the open, straight, and closed faces of a racket. With an open-faced racket you can guarantee that the ball will always strike the front wall above the tin. With a straight or closed head there is a danger that the ball will hit the floor or the tin.

HOW THE RACKET SHOULD STRIKE THE BALL

The natural reaction of most beginners is to face the ball squarely as it comes to them and to scoop it up. This always results in the ball going high. Scooping the ball is a bad habit which should be eliminated. It will be effective only on very rare occasions.

Always keep the grip axis of your racket parallel to the floor of the court, with the head of your racket just above the level of your wrist. (See figures 6 and 7.)

Figure 7.

(a) The behaviour of the ball from an open-faced racket.
(The outlined arrow represents the path of the racket; the solid arrow shows the path of the ball.)
(See figure 7b overleaf.)

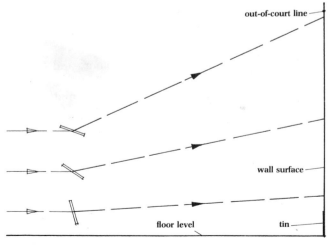

out-of-court line

wall surface

floor level   tin

The grip, the wrist and how the racket strikes the ball   53

(b) Direction of the ball forms a right angle with the racket.

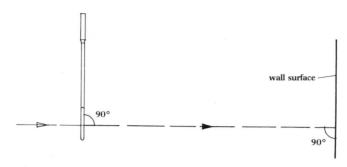

Strike the ball standing sideways on, almost facing the *side* wall: your leading foot — left foot for forehand strokes and right foot for backhand (the reverse for left-handed players) — should point towards the side wall (plate 16). (This stance is explained more fully in Chapter 5.) Train yourself to strike the ball from this position. It applies equally to low or mid-body shots — in fact, all shots.

Always remember that the ball will leave your racket at a right angle, your arm and racket forming one part of the angle, and the flight of the ball the other (see figure 7). This means that you can decide on the height of the shot you want to play simply by adjusting the face of your racket, so altering the angle: fractionally open face — low straight shot; wide open face — a lob.

If the grip axis is parallel to the floor, and the racket is drawn forward in a correct sweep, then the ball will also follow a flight path parallel to the floor; no matter where you are on court, the same rule applies. It works every time.

A collection of different grips, or a single grip which does not keep the racket straight, will not achieve the necessary accuracy.

Plate 16. Correct position for forehand stroke, facing the side wall. Notice how the left foot is leading.

5 · Two very important relationships

YOUR RELATIONSHIP TO THE BALL

When you begin to play, the ball will be cold, without much bounce. But, as you continue striking it, it will warm up. The constant hitting heats it and it warms rapidly, eventually reaching a temperature at which it will become consistent in its behaviour. At this point you can begin to anticipate its performance with confidence.

As the ball bounces it leaves the floor, reaches the top of its bounce, and begins to descend, and that is the best time to hit the ball (figure 8 and plate 21). Why? Because by waiting for this moment, we learn rhythm and timing, develop better judgement, and are better able to evaluate a situation as we gradually grow into the game.

Your mind must be saturated with the rhythm of the ball – it has a music of its own. When calculating the correct time to hit the ball, whether or not it has hit a side wall, you must remember that there is time, time for everything, and no need to hurry. For example, assume that the ball has bounced on the floor and then hit a side wall. The time to hit it is when it comes off the wall, not while it is still on it. The rhythm dictates the timing. It is a universal rule that no two objects can occupy the same space at the same time; therefore, if the ball is on the wall, obviously there is no room for the racket at that same spot. Panicking, smashing the racket against the wall in an effort to scrape the ball off will never achieve the objective. The result will be that the racket takes the place of the ball, trapping it against the wall or sending it to the floor. *Wait!* The ball will eventually come off the wall and leave room for the racket to come through and pick it up.

There is another important factor which we must remember when positioning ourselves for a stroke. *Whether the ball is hit gently or hard, it will cover approximately the same distance between the first and second bounce.* Keeping this in mind, there is no need to rush your shot when your opponent sends a fast ball rocketing towards you. You will still have time to judge the bounce and to position yourself correctly. In other words, treat the fast shot with as much care as you would a slower one.

Rely on these facts, and take advantage of them.

If you take up a position too close to the point where the ball bounced, it will begin its descent (the correct striking position) behind you, as in plate 17. This makes it extremely difficult to play your stroke properly, as you must either wait for the ball to descend to the correct striking point, which means that you will literally have to hit it leaning backwards (plate 17), or rush your shot and hit the ball before it begins to descend.

Another situation which could arise is that although you have placed yourself at the point at which the ball will begin to descend, you have failed to allow enough room between it and you to accommodate the length of your arm and the racket. This leaves you cramped and unbalanced (plate 18).

You should also take into account the fact that standing too far away from the ball will mean that you have to reach for it (as in plate 19) leaving yourself very unbalanced. Since you have a racket in your hand which extends your reach you must instruct your feet to stop at the appropriate distance, which means allowing approximately the length of the racket between you and the ball (plate 20).

You will find the ball difficult to control from any other than the correct position, and you will probably have to be content with just hitting it back as best you can. Note how unbalanced the player is in plates 17, 18 and 19.

Plate 17. Too close to the bounce.

Plate 18. Too close. Not allowing room for the arm and racket.

Plate 19. Reaching for the ball.

Plate 20. Correct distance from the bounce. The player is waiting to the side of the ball, allowing room for his arm, the racket, and the bounce.

Plate 21. Striking point for forehand. The player's position allows for the distance between the bounce and striking point.

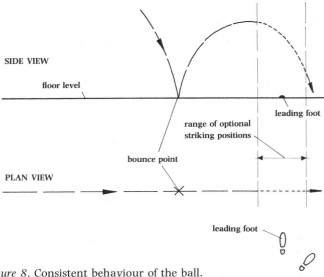

Figure 8. Consistent behaviour of the ball.

These facts are evidence of a living law, which basically describes the relationship between your feet and the ball. You must always observe this law, using your eyes to tell your feet where the ball will bounce. You will then be able to position yourself the correct distance from the bounce and to the side of the ball. This will give you time to execute your shot and enable you to line up your racket, ready to strike the ball.

Approach the ball and *stop moving before you hit it*. Take up your position in relation to the bounce. If you are a right-handed-player, brake with your left foot (leading foot) when playing a forehand stroke (plates 20 and 21).

Do not run at the ball, always approach it from the side.

Striking point

When judging where to stop, you must imagine a line which goes through the length of your left foot. The ball bounces and begins to descend. In its descent, it should cut that line. *That* is the striking point. You can demonstrate it to yourself in the following manner.

Hold the ball in your left hand, arm outstretched, above your left (leading) foot. At the same time, hold your open-faced racket, wrist cocked, ready to make a stroke. Now bring your racket forward slowly to meet the ball in your hand. This is striking point. Maintaining your position, feel for yourself how perfectly it all fits, and how balanced you are.

This small demonstration will help you to understand why, had you stopped in relation to the bounce but too close to the ball, the ball would have hit the shaft of the racket. This forces you to correct the situation by cramping your swing and unbalancing yourself. Conversely, as we have seen, had you stopped too far away from the ball you would have had to reach out for it.

Using this method, we have highlighted the first relationship: your relationship to the ball.

When positioning yourself for the backhand stroke, the situation changes slightly. In playing on the forehand a player has the advantage of his shoulders' width which helps him to use his wrist correctly, and to hit the ball squarely, as shown in plate 21. But when he comes to play backhand, he finds that his racket is already positioned in line with the shoulder nearest the ball. So, in order to achieve the best striking point for the backhand, he must stop with his right foot leading, a shoulders' width farther from the bounce than for the forehand. This will allow him room for wrist action (plate 22). *Do not make the error of striking backhand over your leading foot, you will be striking the ball too far behind you, losing power and balance.*

width of shoulders

Plate 22. Positioning for backhand stroke. Notice the distance of the right foot from striking point, allowing the extra shoulders' width for the player to use his wrist.

THE RELATIONSHIP OF THE BALL TO THE RACKET

The second vital law concerns the relationship between the ball and the racket. Wherever the ball happens to be when descending from the bounce, your racket should be aligned on the same plane ready to strike.

The best striking point differs very slightly from person to person. It depends mainly on the body's configuration, fat or thin, short or tall. You must find the striking point which is most comfortable and easy for you. It will not change any of the principles learned earlier – they remain the same always. As I said earlier, the striking point should be just after the ball starts to complete its dying curve (figure 8). I want you to find out where, within that curve, it is most comfortable for you to strike the ball.

Here are two exercises which will help you to find your own particular striking point.

Stand on the short line by the left wall and, facing the right one, hit the ball to the front wall of the court. When it returns, bounces and begins to descend, position your feet so that the descending ball cuts the imaginary line through your left (leading) foot (figure 8) – left-handed players reverse these instructions. The choice of striking point ranges from immediately the ball starts its descent to just before it hits the floor.

Figure 9. Discovering your striking point by using a lob.

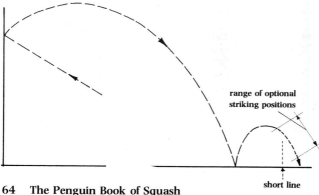

Keep hitting the ball, working your way along the short line to the opposite wall, hitting forehand constantly. When you reach the right-hand wall, turn, and repeat the exercise, using backhand strokes. Note which striking point achieved the best results, and which you felt was most comfortable.

You can gradually train yourself to strike at that same point at all times and whatever the situation. Immediately the habit becomes established, you will have more time to concentrate on tactics, confident that your strokes are correct, and your body well balanced.

You may prefer to discover your best striking point by using a lob, which, being a slower shot, with a higher bounce, allows you more time to decide on the best position for your build (figure 9).

Remember to flex your knees when striking, adopting a slight crouch. The longer you can wait before hitting the ball the better the shot and your timing will be. As long as you keep your racket aligned, and your body correctly balanced, you will be able to send the ball wherever you wish.

Pupil: How high should my racket go when I'm preparing to make a *hard* stroke?

Samir: Your racket must go back as far as is necessary in relation to the height of the ball. Everyone naturally wants to raise the racket high above the shoulder and the head when preparing for a hard shot, but we must be careful not to go too high. Ask other people to watch you during your games and let you know how high and how complicated this part of your stroke is: too high and too complicated will mean a delay in preparing to meet the ball, particularly when you are under pressure. (See plates 23–32.)

6 · The complete forehand and backhand

THE COMPLETE FOREHAND

Plates 23–7. **The complete forehand.**

Plate 23. Note:

 (i) the position of the shoulders;
 (ii) the body has swivelled from the waist;
(iii) the position of the feet does not change: they are facing the side wall;
(iv) eyes on the ball all the time, judging the bounce.

This position is adopted only when you intend to hit your hardest. You have the extra power that comes from the shoulders and from the swivel at the waist.

Plate 23

Plate 24. Notice how the shoulders have swivelled from the waist bringing the arm round. *The arm has not yet been used.* The wrist is *still* right back.

Plate 25. The arm is brought round to position A, where the wrist action begins. It finishes at position B. See plate 26.

NB. Only the arm and the wrist were in action until striking point. *They* have caused the shoulders to come slightly round. You must never use your *whole* body to give you force.

Plate 26. This shows the snap of the wrist which commences at position A and finishes at position B, striking point. Notice how striking point is in line with the left foot.

Plate 27. The follow-through and the pivoting that you see in the picture happen *as* the ball leaves the racket.

THE COMPLETE BACKHAND

Plates 28–32. **The complete backhand.**

Plate 28. Note:

(i) The position of the shoulders;
(ii) the body has swivelled from the waist;
(iii) the position of the feet does not change: they are facing the side wall;
(iv) eyes on the ball all the time, judging the bounce.

As with the forehand, this position is adopted only when you intend to hit your hardest.

Plate 28

Plate 29. Notice how the shoulders have swivelled from the waist bringing the arm round. *The arm has not yet been used*. Notice that the wrist is *still* right back.

Plate 30. The arm is brought to position A.

width of shoulders

B

The arm and the wrist were in action only until striking point. *They* caused the shoulders to come slightly round. Never use your *whole* body to give you momentum.

Plate 31. This shows the snap of the wrist which commences at position A and finishes at position B, striking point.
Notice how striking point is in front of the body leaving a shoulders' width in which to apply the wrist.

Plate 32. The follow-through and pivoting that you see in the picture happen as the ball leaves the racket.

7· Other basic strokes _____

Remember, striking point is always the same, no matter what the stroke or how high the ball. You must always take into account the length of your arm in conjunction with the position of your body while maintaining the same striking point in front of your leading foot.

The big 'S'

The big 'S' is my term for the total range of possible striking points (plates 33–8).

Plates 33–8. **The big 'S' for striking point.**

Plate 33

Plate 34

Plate 35

Plate 36

Plate 37

Plate 38

THE VOLLEY

This is the term used when hitting the ball before it touches the floor. It can be played at any height, and the same two principles must be observed in this stroke as in all others:

1. Assess the striking point, allowing for the length of your racket.

2. Remember the relationship between racket and ball: the racket should be waiting for the ball, wherever it is. (See plates 39 and 40.)

A volley is useful for the following reasons:

(*a*) You can return those high lob serves which eventually end up in the back corner of the court, either leaving you no room to play, or forcing you into a side- or back-wall shot;

(*b*) it is also one of the best methods of pressurizing your partner without unduly rushing yourself. It leaves him less recovery time, and keeps him on his toes.

There are many alternative ways of dealing with the volley. Played softly, it becomes a drop shot (see p. 89), landing in the front of the court. Or, if hit harder, it sails to the back of the court, and achieves 'a good length'. In fact, you retain the freedom to return the ball in whatever manner you choose, taking into account the position in which your partner has placed himself.

Make it a hard and fast rule always to volley when the opportunity arises.

Plates 39–40 (overleaf). **The volley, forehand and backhand.**

Notice how the racket is in front of the leading foot, linked and waiting for the ball.

In the forehand, striking point is in front of the left foot.
In the backhand, striking point is a shoulders' width in front of the right foot.

Plate 39

Plate 40

THE HALF VOLLEY

This entails hitting the ball after the bounce when it is only an inch or two from the floor, without waiting for it to rise and descend as you would in the normal way. (See plate 41.)

As it is an immediate, very low level stroke, its effects on your partner are the same as those achieved by volleying. Again, you can play it as a soft or a hard stroke, but it is more usually a soft shot. It can be used on those occasions where you would have liked to volley, but were unable to reach the ball in time. It is basically a surprise shot, in that it ruins your opponent's anticipation and timing.

Plate 41. **The half volley (forehand).** Striking point is still in front of the leading foot.

THE DROP SHOT (*figure 10*)

The drop shot is played by striking the ball gently from any part of the court and causing it to land at the front of the court, hitting the front wall just above the tin. The reason for playing this shot is to make your opponent run from one end of the court to the other, having manoeuvred him out of position before playing your shot.

Your racket should be lined up level with the ball, your wrist cocked (racket head above the wrist), as the ball descends from the bounce. Strike it with a gentle touch of the wrist and an open-faced racket. Direct it to either of the front corners.

NOTE: Your feet dictate the angle of the ball. See the position that has been adopted in plate 42 (overleaf) to direct the ball to the left-hand corner.

Figure 10. The drop shot.

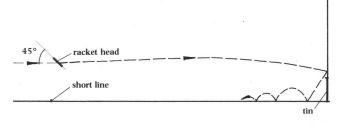

Plate 42. **The drop shot.** The ball is directed towards the left corner of the front wall (approximately 2 ft (60 cm) from that corner and just above the tin).

THE SIDE-WALL SHOT (THE BOAST) (*figure 11*)

This is a shot played on to the side wall, and may be either defensive or attacking, depending on the circumstances. To play it, the ball must be directed at the side wall at an angle that will cause it to rebound eventually to the front wall. This is one of the main ways of playing the ball out of difficult corners. It can also be used to wrong foot an opponent: if he has anticipated a straight shot, and has begun to move before you have played your ball, you can use the walls to place your shot behind him.

When you become completely at home on the court, you will find that the walls can be your best friends because, if you abide by the rules, they will never let you down.

The following diagram shows how, using the walls, you can get yourself out of otherwise impossible situations.

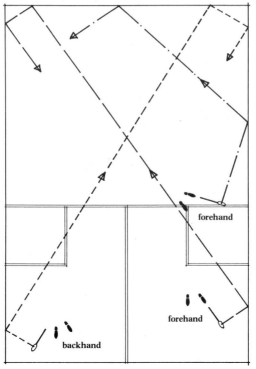

Figure 11.
The side-wall shot.
Notice the angles
which are formed
within the
rectangular
environment of
the court.

THE LOB

To lob the ball is to hit it so that it goes in a high arc, not only above your opponent's head, but above his outstretched racket also, thereby forcing him to follow the ball to the back of the court. This gives you time to make your recovery, especially if you have been pressed into a tight situation at the front. You can, however, play a lob from any part of the court, always keeping your racket head open to ensure that the ball travels high (plates 43 and 44).

Plates 43–4. **The lob, forehand and backhand.** The grip axis is parallel to the floor and the face of the racket is wide open.

THE BACK-WALL SHOT (*figure 12*)

This is a purely defensive shot, only to be used when your opponent has left you no alternative. It is, in effect, a lob played on to the back wall in such a manner (wide open face and plenty of wrist) that the ball will sail high over the court and eventually hit the front wall. Because the ball takes quite a while to cover this distance, it gives your opponent plenty of time to reach it and 'put it away' while you are still returning from the back of the court. It should be used only *in extremis* to keep you in the game (plate 45).

Figure 12. The back-wall shot.

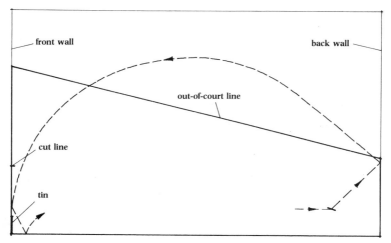

Plate 45. **The back-wall shot.** The face of the racket is wide open. Hardly any arm is required, but plenty of wrist.

8 · The service _____

As is the case with all racket sports, good service is the foundation of success, although most players are unaware of its importance and do not realize that by playing a good serve they can gain an advantage over their partner.

There are several different methods of serving, all good, and well suited to those players that favour them. My feelings on the subject are, however, that a player who can vary his service throughout any one match will benefit more than the one who develops a particular type of service and invariably uses it. My reasoning is that, no matter how good that service is, eventually the opposing player will be able to analyse it and deal with it. Whereas, if you keep several different serves in your repertoire, your partner will be unable to anticipate you, and may find that, unless he keeps on his toes, he is caught in the wrong position and is totally unable to deal with your delivery.

This is why, so often, the odd bad service can win a point, because it is unexpected. One can learn a valuable lesson from this; never assume that your partner will always serve the same type of ball. When waiting to receive, watch him closely, all the time, as this may help you to anticipate the sort of serve he plans to play, either by his positioning, or by the way he drops the ball on to the racket. Either way, you will be bound to learn a lot more than you would by having your eyes glued to the front wall.

Another very important point: practise serving equally from either side of the court, backhand as well as forehand.

Although you are able to choose whichever serving box you prefer when first becoming 'hand in', on successive serves you must alternate between both, and it would be foolish to concentrate mainly on your forehand serve, only to fail when forced to serve from the backhand court. If you take into account the fact that your opponent is probably stronger when receiving on his forehand, it is logical to concentrate on your backhand service, rather more than on your forehand. Remember, you are almost certain to meet a left-hander somewhere in your career, who will be extremely grateful if your service from the backhand box is weak and ineffectual. My main advice on serving is, therefore, to be versatile.

Figure 13. The area to aim for in service.

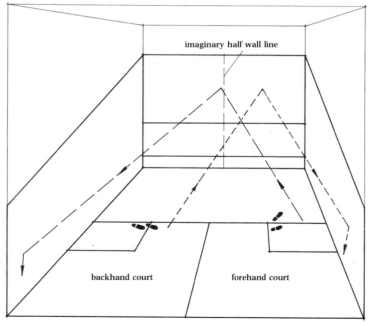

PREPARING TO SERVE

When serving from the forehand box, the whole width of the court is within range, so that you can aim for the middle of the front wall, or just off centre, but when serving from the backhand court the angle is narrowed. This means that you must aim for the centre of the farthest half of the front wall to achieve the correct flight path and angle (figure 13).

Where should you stand to serve?

In my experience, and this is borne out by the majority of internationals, the best position is that shown in figure 13.

THE LOB SERVICE (*figure 14*, p. 100)

Note the following points:

(*a*) the feet are lined up to form a right angle with the direction of the ball;

(*b*) the racket also forms a right angle with the direction of the ball;

(*c*) alignment of the racket and ball;

(*d*) face of the racket is, in this case, wide open, to produce a lob service;

(*e*) the ball is held initially in the hand, approximately one foot (30 cm) above waist level.

Striking the ball (*plates* 47 and 48)

In order to produce the angle that you require:

1. bring your racket and wrist as far back as is comfortable – for the soft service illustrated here just use the arm slightly to create momentum;

2. when you are ready and balanced, let the ball drop in line with the striking point that you have mentally established, ensuring that, when you snap your wrist to strike, you meet the ball at waist level;

Plates 46–50. **The lob service.**

  (i) Note the position of the feet and the angle that they make.
 (ii) Note how the racket and the ball are lined up.
(iii) The face of the racket is wide open to produce a lob.

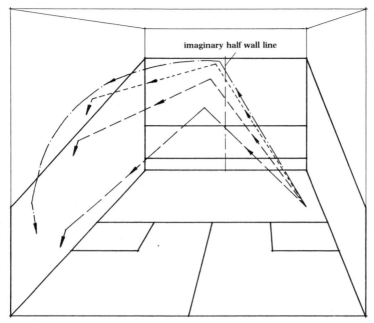

Figure 14. The higher the softer.

3. make sure that your racket is sufficiently open to produce the lob that you require.

The follow-through

You must follow through with your racket in order to produce accuracy, and to avoid reducing the velocity of the ball (plate 49).

1. Your eyes must follow the ball all the way from your own to your partner's racket. Immediately after the ball leaves your racket you must pivot so that you are able to watch your partner and make for the T area as well. This will allow you to adopt a good strategic position for dealing with his return (plate 50).

Plate 47. The racket is taken back in preparation for the stroke. The wrist is bent back. Mentally, the link between the racket and the ball is being established.

Plate 48. The racket is brought forward, meeting the ball at striking point.

Plate 49. The follow-through.

Plate 50. Pivoting, following the ball, watching your opponent, anticipating where he will send the ball.

2. Watch him preparing to strike. Try to see where he will aim his ball. This will preclude your being taken by surprise and will give you sufficient time to pass the message to your feet.

3. You must remember to follow the ball with your eyes constantly, as this keeps you in time with its rhythm and aware of all that may be happening.

The aim of the lob service is to lift the ball above the opponent's racket and force him to the back corners of the court. As with most things, it takes practice to become consistent, and, unless faultlessly executed, this serve can deliver a soft, high ball directly to your opponent's racket, one that he can volley without too much effort. But it is generally accepted that, when played well, this is one of the most difficult services to return.

When playing the lob, there is no need to hit the ball hard. Indeed, if you hit it too hard, there is a real danger that it will go out of court. A firm stroke will lift the ball so that it strikes the front wall slightly off centre, just below the out-of-court line. It will then sail high in a loop and slide down the side wall near the rear of the court.

If you find that your serve is not following the required route, adjust the position of your feet and experiment until you find that exact point on the front wall which gives you the angle you are looking for.

A basic rule to remember, whether or not you are serving, is: the higher the softer. In other words, the higher you intend hitting the wall, the more softly you hit the ball. For a lob serve, you aim for the wall just below the out-of-court line, and, in these circumstances, had you not struck the ball gently, it would have been out of court by the time it reached the side wall.

For a fast service, you aim the ball so that it hits the front wall just above the cut line and, because it keeps low, you can hit it hard. Figure 14 illustrates the point. You must be conscious of the court's angles and their effect on your ball at all times.

I have described the lob service first because it is a serve which can be used quite easily by beginners. Of course the absolute beginner will be relieved if he can just serve a ball which lands within his opponent's quarter. He does not yet have the experience required to hit a low fast serve, or indeed, to place his service with any great accuracy.

Please do not place too much importance on your serve at first; it will suffice if you can just get the ball into play. Don't worry either about your partner's opinion of your service at this early stage. If you are fortunate enough to have a partner who is learning as well, he will be in no position to criticize anyway. If a more experienced player has agreed to come on court with you for a while, then he will undoubtedly be patient and understanding, remembering the time when he was in your position.

The lob is the easiest then, because it requires little force. Just a tap with an open-faced racket and a flick of the wrist will ensure that the ball is lifted sufficiently to return to the opposite quarter of the court.

As you progress, you will find that other services become possible, and you will want to incorporate them in your game. This saves you from becoming typecast. Everyone has their own favourite service – it is very much a matter of personal preference – but remember always to keep your opponent guessing.

THE FAST SERVE

As shown in figure 14 the fast service should be played so that its impact on the front wall is just above the cut line. The positioning of your feet will remain the same as for the lob, since the angle of the four walls is unchanged. The only change is in the speed of your delivery, and the height of impact on the front wall.

Because you want the ball to follow a lower trajectory, the face of your racket should be only fractionally open, as opposed to the lob where the face is wide open. A faster snap of the wrist will impart greater speed to your ball. Don't forget to follow through. The ball will follow the path indicated by the diagrams, striking the side wall within the opposite quarter of the court.

The fast serve sometimes gives the added bonus of surprising your partner into a silly shot. The speed of your delivery encourages him to rush his return instead of taking his time and playing the stroke properly. Alternatively, the fact that the ball is travelling so fast means that, if he keeps his head, all he has to do is to hold his racket out to meet the ball correctly, and, with very little effort on his part, he can perform a perfect drop shot return. Bearing this in mind, never rest on your laurels after playing a scorching service — be prepared for an equally superb return.

If you wish to vary the spot at which the served ball hits the side wall after leaving the front, alter the position of your feet very slightly. This will change the angle of flight, without changing the striking point, which is always in front of your leading toe.

The decision as to where you send your ball should always be dictated by the position of your partner. Everyone has a blind spot; try to find his. If he is the sort of player who tends to stand near the back corner when receiving service, place your ball so that it cuts across his body, pinning him there. This will make him quite ineffectual, and demoralize him completely.

Squash is as much a mental battle as a physical one. You can overpower an opponent as easily by finding his weaknesses as by outplaying him with superior shots.

The variations of service are of course up to you. Find your own favourites, perfect them, and use them. Try to discover early in the game which of your services is giving your opponent the most trouble, and use it only until he appears to have got your measure. Then pop in a different one, so destroying any confidence which he may have felt.

THE CHAMPIONS' SERVE

You may occasionally see, or have thrown at you during a match, a service which is only generally used by extremely experienced players. The fact that it is only rarely used is not only because it is difficult to execute, but also because it is very difficult for a marker to judge.

The method is to serve the ball with a backhand stroke from the forehand box, at such an angle that it hits the front wall just below the out-of-court line in the top right-hand corner. It goes to the side wall at a very narrow angle, and then flies across court, very high, crossing the opposite back quarter in the area of the unfortunate opponent's head (figure 15).

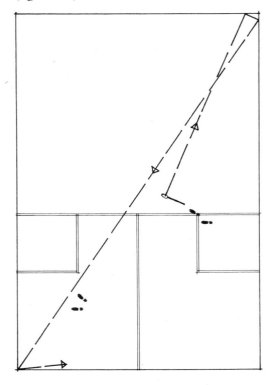

Figure 15.
The champions'
serve.

The beauty of this service is its element of surprise, especially if it is the first time during a match that it has been played.

Until you become highly skilled, and feel confident that you can perform this kind of service without 'faulting', content yourself with watching and marvelling at the champions. There are several far safer services available to you.

WHEN YOU SERVE A FAULT

If you play a faulted service — one which does not land in your opponent's quarter — never make the mistake of relaxing and assuming that he will not play it. He is entitled to do so if he chooses, even if it is a 'fault'. As long as the ball does not go out of court, he is free to play any ball even if it does not land within his area. So be prepared.

If you serve a fault, and he decides not to take it, then you may serve again. If you serve a fault the second time, you lose service, and your opponent becomes 'hand in'. Alternatively, if he takes a swing at a faulted service and fails to make a correct return, he cannot then object, claiming that it was a 'bad' serve. Once he can be said to have played the ball, he has lost any right to object.

9·Basic tactics _____

BECOMING A PART OF YOUR ENVIRONMENT

When people come to me for coaching, their first lesson generally comes as something of a surprise to them. We have the usual warm up, just hitting the ball to one another, forehand and backhand, during which time I am assessing the standard and type of person I am dealing with.

Then I ask that they try to become a part of the environment, allow the court to grow on them, so that they will feel at home there. They must come to know it as well as their own homes, where they can find their way about in the dark, missing the furniture and the angles because they know exactly where everything is instinctively.

I point out the four consistent factors:

> the court
> the racket
> the ball
> the design of the human body.

I go on to indicate the court's dimensions and the position of the out-of-court lines. We look at the racket and discuss the fact that although the weight can vary the performance is always the same; I explain that the bounce of the ball is consistent, whatever its speed. I stress that the relevant information should be passed from the mind to the body.

All that remains is for them to discover how to exploit the

relevant factors, making them complement each other, and taking advantage of a complete knowledge and understanding of the environment.

The design of the court makes it obvious why we do things a certain way: why we hold the racket the way we do, and why we use the same grip at all times; why we keep the grip axis parallel to the floor in order to maintain accuracy and consistency. There is no alternative. Because of the court's structure, the positions of the tin and the boundary lines, and, more important, the build of the human body, this method of striking the ball is the only one which will guarantee success.

When my students become aware of all the factors, and thoroughly understand them, they are then ready to go on and discover for themselves the correct way to bring them into harmony, always bearing in mind the all-important laws and the reasons behind them. Only in this way can success be assured.

Court tactics are simply a product of your 'court feel'. When the environment has become a second home to you, you will quickly learn to place yourself strategically in order to make the best of yourself. The behaviour of the ball and its relation to the walls become inevitable to one who understands the reasons for them. You will always be able to position yourself correctly in order to hit the ball, and you will have sufficient time to decide on how best to place the ball so that it will cause the most inconvenience to your opponent.

The ability to move around freely and confidently within this environment is a major part of the game: knowing when and where to move is therefore second nature to the good player. You can train yourself to think and act simultaneously, so that you move with fluidity and with the minimum waste of effort.

Your mind must be thinking, alert and watchful. I can only give you guidelines. You must make independent decisions based on the type of person you are. Positioning is imperative: you must remain one jump ahead. Keep questioning your senses. Where is your partner? Where is the ball? Where are you?

TACTICS

The best tactic for beginners is that of putting one short ball to the front of the court, and then one to the back. One to the left, and one to the right. This is the furthest you can expect your thoughts to stretch at this stage. Remember always to give your partner a fair view of the ball, and to give yourself a fair view of him, and you will not go far wrong. Treat squash as a game of chess, always anticipating the next move, and forcing your partner to play your game.

I have included here a few samples of route and positioning; it would be virtually impossible to give all the permutations, but I feel that those shown are the basic ones, and will give you something on which to build. You will note that in my examples I do not advocate standing exactly on the bar of the T, but within an area slightly to the side. If you stand here your opponent's body will not block your view of his racket when he strikes the ball — which you must see in order to anticipate his next shot.

Follow these basic tactics and you will keep out of trouble. Advanced tactics come much later in your career, when your shots and court knowledge are more developed. I plan to cover tactics up to championship level in my next book, and do not feel that they are necessary at this stage.

RETURNING SERVICE

I propose to spend some time discussing the different methods of returning service. I have listed the returns in the order in which I would recommend them.

Any stroke consists, in fact, of two parts: the first part, actually hitting the ball, and the second, the follow-through of your body, which is preparing to move on in a chosen direction. The two parts cannot be separated: the second must always follow as an integral part of the first. Both combined make one continuous and fluid movement. Any hesitation will cost you a fraction of a second which you can ill afford. You must train yourself to think on the move. Watch your opponent as intently as the predator watches his prey.

The first diagram of each pair shows the path taken by the ball. The second — the avoidance pattern diagram — illustrates the second stage of the shot. This is a little more complex; it involves moving into the ideal position to deal with your opponent's shot. The diagram shows your eventual position and the route which you should take to get there.

Avoidance pattern — get out of your opponent's way and leave him plenty of room. Master this and you have mastered the 'let' problem. (For more about the 'let' problem, see p. 151.)

In my opinion, the best way of returning service is that shown in figure 16, my reasons being that it is safe and effective, and can therefore be recommended with confidence to the beginner and the intermediate player.

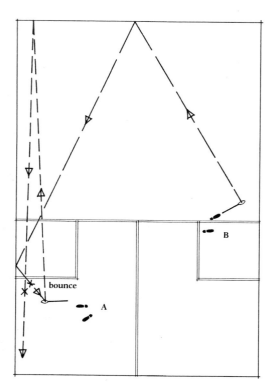

Figure 16.

(a) Service and return no. 1. Hit the ball so that it comes back parallel to the side wall nearest to you, hugging the wall (the closer the better), and bounces near the back line of the service box. This will ensure that it 'dies' on or near the nick formed by the back wall and the floor. If your ball bounces any farther back, you run the risk of it coming off the back wall, thus giving your opponent time to collect it on the rebound. Your knowledge of distance and length will help you to judge just how much power is required to bring the ball back to the ideal position.

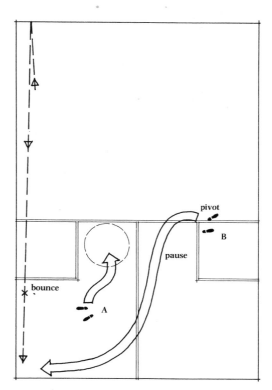

(b) Avoidance pattern no. 1. Server B plays and prepares for next shot. He turns and moves into the T area which affords him a good view of A, pauses, sees the direction of the ball and moves down court.

'Hand out' A plays shot and moves up to T area; watches B.

The second method of returning service is to hit the ball back parallel to the side wall. The ball must:

1. hit the wall just above the tin;
2. be hard and fast;
3. bounce in the front part of the court as shown in figure 17a.

In other words, it is a brisk and surprising shot and very difficult to return.

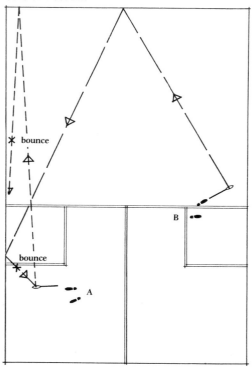

Figure 17.

(a) Service and return no. 2. Send the ball down the same wall, the one nearest to you, but, by using more wrist in your stroke, increase the speed so that the ball rebounds from the front wall extremely quickly. This will harass and pressurize your opponent.

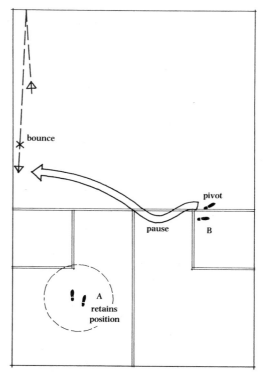

(b) Avoidance pattern no. 2. B pivots and watches, making as much ground as possible. Anticipates return and moves to play. A remains within the same general area as it gives a good view of B's racket.

The third method of returning service is the drop shot (figures 18 and 19). Regardless of whether you play it from a high volley, or wait until after the ball has bounced, you must place the ball low in either of the front corners. This will leave your opponent very little time to reach the ball before it 'dies'.

The reason why I have listed this type of return after the others is that any error of judgement will result in the ball hitting the tin, so ending the rally in your partner's favour.

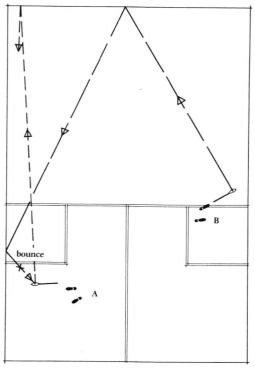

bounce

B

A

Figure 18.

(a) Service and return no. 3 — drop shot return into nearside corner. Regardless of whether you play from a high volley, or wait until after the ball has bounced, you must place the ball low in either of the front corners.

It certainly does not mean that I do not approve of the drop shot return; indeed, I personally rate this type of shot higher than any other and almost invariably use it myself. But you must remember that I have practised for many years, so that, with concentration, I am able to complete it perfectly almost every time. But I would advise anyone who does not have this confidence to use the safe returns until the drop shot has been practised to near-perfection.

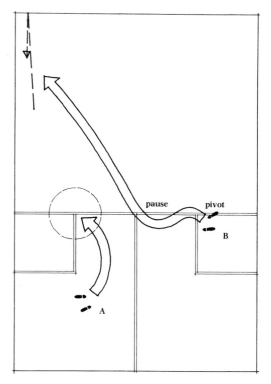

(b) Avoidance pattern no. 3 – B pivots and moves into T area. Pauses and, anticipating A's return, moves quickly up court. A moves into area shown ready to move either across or down court, depending on B's next move.

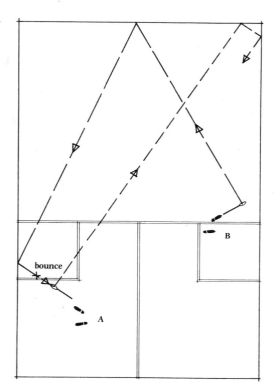

Figure 19.

(a) Service and return no. 3a – drop shot return to far corner.

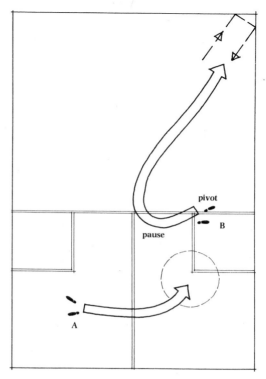

pivot

pause

B

A

(b) Avoidance pattern no. 3a. B moves into T area and pauses to watch, trying to anticipate where A plans to place his ball. Following the ball, he moves up the court to meet it. After playing return, A moves into a position which allows him a good view of B's racket.

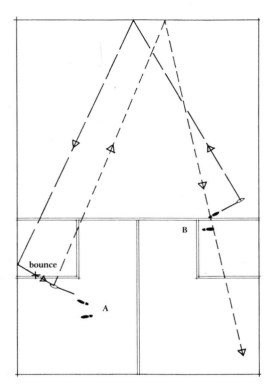

bounce

B

A

Figure 20.

(a) Service and return no. 4. The ball must be played so that it goes high over the server's head, forcing him back into the far corner of the court.

The last return on my list is the lob (figure 20). The ball must be played so that it goes high over the server's head, forcing him back into the far corner of the court. Anything low enough for him to reach is a waste of time as he will be able to volley it and possibly win the rally. It is the most difficult return to make, and the danger of failure is great. It requires a lot of practice, at least twice that needed for any other shot. But, if you are already able to serve a good lob consistently, you could attempt it, using the same technique.

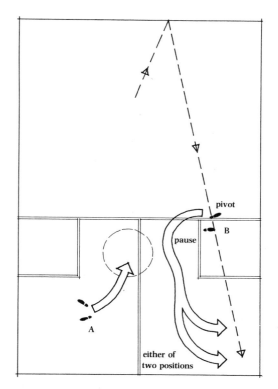

pivot

B

pause

either of
two positions

A

(b) Avoidance pattern no. 4. After service B turns into the T area
and pauses, watching A. He carries on, in an almost continuous
movement, to the rear of the court. The two positions shown in
the diagram are dependent upon whether he decides to volley the
ball, or to wait until it returns from the back wall. A moves into
the area shown, keeping B in view and his eyes on the ball.

The difference is, of course, that when serving you choose
your own time to play, whereas when receiving you have
less thinking time. But, providing that your timing is as it
should be, this will not cause you any problems.

BELIEVE IT OR NOT!

To practise these returns and to learn to play them with confidence, refer back to figure 7 and pp. 53–5.

If you follow the rules I have given you you will be able to hit the wall consistently just above the tin. *Whatever the height of the ball when you hit it,* the head of the racket must always move parallel to the floor, in a straight line, and come through level with the ball; the racket must always be fractionally open-faced.

Correct training is as valuable here as years of experience – there are international players who will admit that they cannot guarantee that they will hit the wall immediately above the tin, yet I have students who can do it with confidence although they are still beginners. Indeed, one club has recently had to repair the front wall of the court which we use for coaching – constant wear had made a groove in the plaster just above the tin!

10 · False concepts _____

I have included this short chapter to correct some of the errors frequently made by beginners. They are not serious, and can be cleared up quite quickly.

(a) One of the most common mistakes made by beginners is the feeling that a very fast shot is impossible to connect with, let alone control. This concept is totally false, although understandable. As long as you remember and follow the principles learned earlier, relating the ball to the racket and the feet, you will find that if you place yourself correctly, the ball will hit your waiting racket, and zing off with no effort at all.

Even very young children ask me for 'whizzie ones' because they are great fun to return, and they have discovered that they were afraid of something that only lived in their imagination. Do not allow yourself to be intimidated by a hard shot, just play your return the correct way. You will be surprised when you see the result.

(b) Another false concept often held is that a player feels bound to hit a hard shot equally hard in return, when in fact it would probably be preferable to treat the shot with contempt, hitting it gently, and placing it in the front of the court. Very annoying for your opponent, especially if he had been confident that his shot was so fast that it had to be a winner. Never be afraid of a hard-hitting player. Keep cool, and make him play your game.

(c) When hitting the ball to the side or back wall some players may feel that they need to hit it hard as it is the only way of making it reach the front wall — another misconception. In order to move the ball, all you need to do is keep your racket face open, and hit it gently, using your wrist and remaining the correct distance from the striking point. It's all in the snap of the wrist. Once mastered, I guarantee that you will play a better shot than you ever thought possible — relaxed and controlled, enabling you to prepare for the next shot, instead of being exhausted from the energy you expended on the last one.

(d) There is a very common misunderstanding regarding the different coloured dots on the squash ball. The balls are available in varying degrees of pace in order to suit the temperature and conditions of the court on which the game is to be played. They are graded so that, regardless of court temperature, they will play consistently, covering the same distance between bounces. The blue dot ball, for instance, warms up very quickly, and becomes extremely lively when struck repeatedly with any force. It would eventually become almost uncontrollable on a warm court. Alternatively, the yellow dot is slow to heat, and, after reaching a certain level, will remain consistent on a warm court. So, when choosing your ball, consider the conditions of the court: if the court is centrally heated, use a yellow dot ball; if it is a cold court, use a white dot ball.

Balls bearing the red or blue dot should only be used when playing on a freezing cold court, or by beginners who are still having difficulty in connecting with the ball at all — people who do not have enough power to warm up the slow balls. Once a beginner has learnt to hit the ball, he should choose the correct one according to court conditions, not to what he considers is his standard of play.

I have raised this point with the manufacturers, and, in the absence of any definite ruling from them as to whether the ball should be chosen for court conditions or playing standards, I make this assertion on the basis of my own experience.

THE T AREA (*figure 21*)

Everybody seems to advise players to move to the T regardless, after playing their shot. The false concept begins when whoever gives the advice fails to qualify it. The shot which you

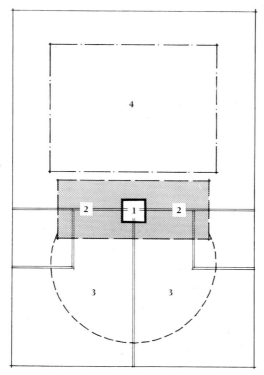

Figure 21. The T area.

1. The traditional T area.

2. The area that I recommend as the T. You will usually be positioned here awaiting your opponent's return shot.

3. You would position yourself somewhere in this area if you felt certain that your opponent would be returning your shot to the back of the court.

4. You would wait in this area if you felt certain that your opponent would have to return your shot either off the back wall or the side wall. In either case the ball will land in the front of the court.

have just played will determine the area of the court in which you should be positioned to receive your opponent's return. I hope figures 16 to 21 will help to clear up this anomaly.

I will begin by quoting an extreme example, to show that the principle cannot hold on all occasions. If, for example, you played a bad shot towards the centre of the court, and, after striking, you moved to the T, you would almost inevitably clash with your partner who should already be there. Obviously on this occasion you would be unable to go to the T. So what do you do? Settle for the nearest you can get? But while jockeying for position you may well have missed getting a good view of his shot.

Why, then, is this principle so frequently stressed? It is mainly to give a prod to those people who forget to move after playing their shot, and who need some guideline. Please do not misunderstand me; the T is undoubtedly the prime area, but the area stretches far wider than the actual bars of the T. You must place yourself within that area, but in a position where you can see your partner, and can read his next shot, no matter where he is.

You must learn to move away so that you do not hinder him but can still see his racket meet the ball. If you are in harmony with the bounce, you will be able to judge where he must be to meet the correct striking point and place yourself accordingly.

The T is only a landmark for a much larger area. You will see in the avoidance pattern diagrams (figures 16–20) that the positions I have designated for our imaginary players are often well outside that part of the court generally called the T, but that they are always in a position which allows them a good view of the ball, without blocking their partner, and that they can, if anticipating correctly, reach any part of the court in which he chooses to place his ball.

I feel, therefore, that mindlessly returning to the T bar is to be discouraged; be aware of the principle, but remember, too, that if by being there you have effectively blocked your view you will have lost valuable time, as you will only be able to judge the ball's direction after it has left the wall.

11 · Orientation

Your feeling for the lines and landmarks of the court should become as automatic as breathing. You will obviously endeavour to travel the shortest distance between points, if possible, while giving your opponent as much room as he needs. Knowledge of distance and area is important; spend time on court by yourself, learning to assimilate all the landmarks, and letting the surroundings grow on you. This will mean that after a time you will be able to put yourself on automatic pilot, leaving your subconscious to do the thinking while you concentrate on your shots. This is called court orientation. The landmarks are as follows:

1. Corners: they make angles — use them to change the direction of the ball.

2. The T area, as marked on the diagrams: this is the area to aim for as it is the ideal strategic position, and gives you a good view of your opponent's stroke.

3. Rear line of the service boxes: the danger area for the bounce, and a guideline for you — a ball bouncing here is the signal for you to hustle.

4. The short line: this effectively halves the court and is a helpful orientation line.

5. The half court line: it quarters the court, dividing it into forehand and backhand.

6. Out-of-court lines: practise hitting your ball just under the upper line, and just above the tin until, subconsciously, you know exactly where they are. Just as in darts you learn where the numbers are on the board, so in squash you must know where the markings are.

7. The ceiling: check the height of the ceiling and of any beams or hanging light fittings which may affect your lob and high-flight balls. This should become a part of your consciousness whenever you are a guest in a strange club.

PRACTICE EXERCISES

The following exercises are intended to assist in orientation. They will help you to judge the effects of all of the constant factors.

Exercise 1

Practise forehand and backhand strokes as shown in plates 51–5. When practising these two strokes, learn to develop the *grip*, to use your *wrist*, and to apply the two relationships. Putting them into practice helps you to develop *stance*, *rhythm*, and *timing*. This exercise must be practised against a side wall; the idea is to force you to hit the ball gently.

Exercise 2

Practise hitting the ball forehand and backhand *on the volley*. In this exercise, you will learn how intensely one needs to concentrate. Keep your eyes on the ball, and your mind on the job. This is a superb exercise for waking one up.

Exercise 3 (*figure 22*)

Face the front and hit a lob high up on a side wall, one which will curve overhead to the opposite side wall, bounce on the floor, and return to the playing position, forming a con-

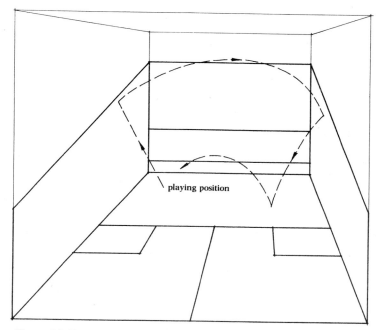

playing position

Figure 22. Exercise 3.

tinuous circle overhead. Keep the ball going. This is a fairly difficult exercise at first, but it will help your service and your timing, and teach you to keep the racket face open. More important, you will discover that there is only one correct striking point which will keep the ball under control. This can only be learned by experience. Try it on forehand and backhand.

Exercise 4 (*figure 23*)

Stand in the middle of the court on the T. Hit the ball forehand towards the front wall, angling it so that it hits the wall near the corner, and so goes on to the side wall, eventually coming back to where you are standing.

Change your stance while the ball is in flight so that when it returns you are ready to hit it backhand towards the

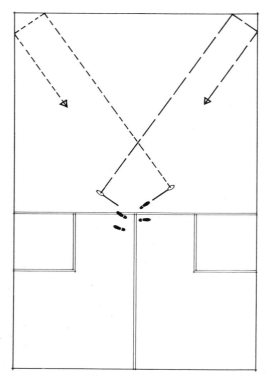

Figure 23. Exercise 4.

opposite corner, using the same angle, so that it will return again.

Repeat. Count the number of strokes you can play without a break, forehand and backhand alternately. This exercise will not only train you to watch the ball, but also to move your feet into the correct position automatically.

Use your wrist and keep the racket face open, grip axis parallel to the floor. There is no trick in it, you either follow the rhythm or lose control of the ball. Even so, it is not as easy as it looks because it demands a long spell of concentration and good coordination. (Figure 23 illustrates the position of your racket and feet.)

Exercise 5 (*figures 24–5*)

Stand in the back quarter of the court, about two feet (60 cm) behind the serving box. Hit the ball directly to the front wall, prepare for its return, and play a drop shot to the opposite front corner, across court. Direct the ball at such an angle that it hits the front wall, then the side wall, and comes rolling back to you. This saves a lot of walking.

Practise both forehand and backhand, noting the gentle wrist action, the angle of approach to the ball and the degree of open face on your racket. Also note where the striking point is relative to your feet, and the height at which your racket should be waiting.

Figure 24. Exercise 5: the forehand drop shot.

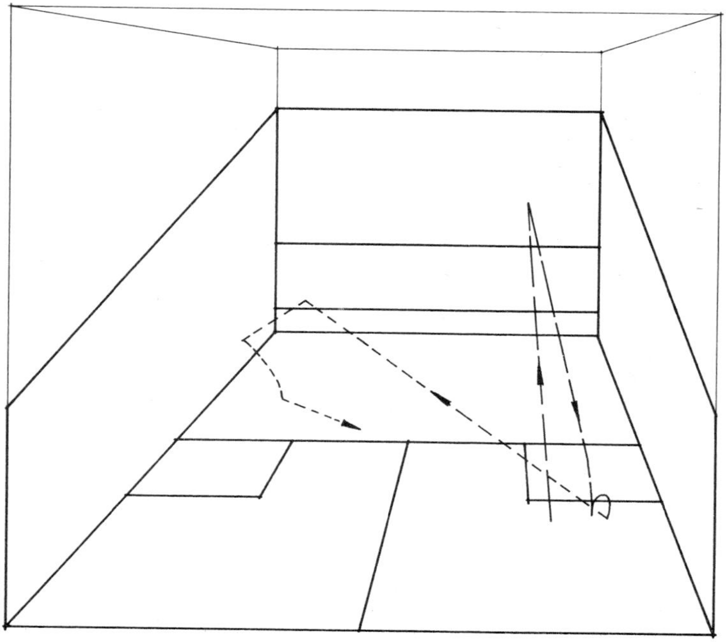

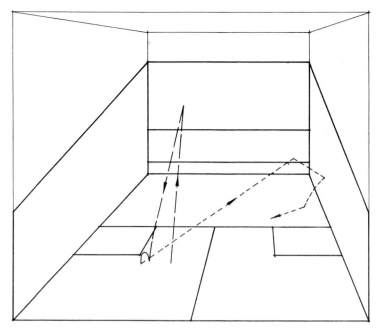

Figure 25. Exercise 5: the backhand drop shot.

Exercise 6 (*figure 26*)

Stand in the middle of the court by the bars of the T. Serve yourself a lob and volley it forehand into the left front corner. Once again, if you angle it correctly, the ball will hit the side wall and return across the floor. Pick it up with your racket, and lob it again. This time, when it returns, volley it backhand into the other corner.

This exercise teaches patience; the ball must be watched closely to ensure that the racket is waiting at the correct height and striking point. It will also help you to deal with those difficult serves which give the very best players some trouble, for unless you return that sort of serve in the manner described in this exercise, the ball will probably die in the back corner.

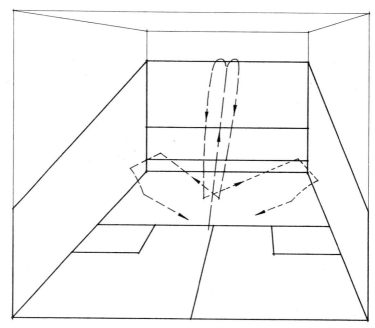

Figure 26. Exercise 6.

You will be amazed at the results of practising this exercise, and at the ease with which it can be achieved.

Exercise 7

This is an exercise for two people, standing on opposite sides of the court, hitting the ball back and forth. The exercise consists of each person endeavouring to make his ball bounce within the opposite serving box. Every time he succeeds, he gains a point. The same applies to his opponent. It is quite easy, although it requires good judgement to be able to find the right spot consistently, which of course, is the whole point of the exercise – the scoring is simply a way of making it more challenging and of measuring your progress.

Exercise 8 (*figure 27*)

For this exercise, you will have to invent imaginary floor markings, as shown in the diagram. Your playing area will consist only of the area down one wall, stretching from the wall itself out to a line which is a continuation of the far edge of the serving box. This leaves you with a long, narrow court. The players are allowed to step outside this area but the ball is restricted to the reduced court. You and your partner stand behind the half court line, facing the side wall alongside each other. The player nearest the front wall serves. The served ball must fall behind the half court line as in a normal game. Once 'hand in' has served the ball so that it returns down that wall he must move away, allowing his partner room to play a shot.

Figure 27. Exercise 8.

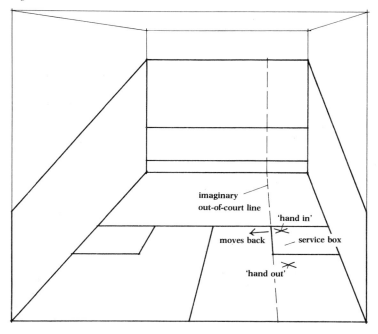

imaginary
out-of-court line

'hand in'

moves back   service box

'hand out'

Use the normal scoring system. This exercise will help you to move away from, and around, your opponent. By diminishing the playing area, we highlight foot-dragging and so become more nimble. Any type of shot is allowed as long as the ball does not leave the playing area. Apart from developing agility, this exercise gives a great deal of amusement. It can be played on the backhand and forehand court. Learn to play in close proximity to the wall — this dispels wall shyness. Note that 'hand out' is standing approximately three feet (1 m) behind the serving box in order to give his partner serving room.

Exercise 9 (*figure 28*)

Once again, we must imagine a new out-of-court line, this time one which stretches across the court, about five or six feet (2 m) from the front wall. It helps if you mark the boundary by placing some objects on the imaginary line close to the side wall. The players take up positions facing the front wall, one on each side of the court.

The usual rules apply; the elected server choosing the side from which he will serve, and alternating sides until he becomes 'hand out'. The ball is served to the side wall, hitting the front and opposite side wall (in any order) before bouncing. In other words, a three-wall serve. Anything less means loss of service.

The game can then begin with each player trying to outwit, and at the same time not collide with, his partner. The narrow playing area means that, of necessity, any shots you play must be either narrow angle or drop shots. This exercise, therefore, develops touch and finesse.

Most people manage the three-wall service fairly quickly on the forehand, but not quite so quickly on the backhand, as when serving on the right-hand side of the court you have to serve the ball with a backhand stroke.

The secret is to throw the ball under, and not too close to, your waiting racket, leaving enough room for your arm and wrist to sweep through to connect with it. It does take practice, but it is a useful skill, so do persevere.

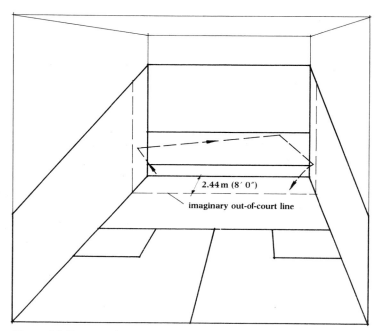

2.44 m (8′ 0″)

imaginary out-of-court line

Figure 28. Exercise 9.

I have done my best to develop exercises which are not only beneficial, but interesting and enjoyable. They will all help to increase your awareness of the court, and of yourself within this environment, therefore making you feel at home within your surroundings. There are many other exercises which you could try; you could invent some yourself, as I have. The ones I have given you are the ones that I give to my students, and, although very basic, they are ideal for teaching those principles which must be learned. They will also help to prove that observing these principles is the only way to succeed consistently in squash, and that they apply no matter who you are, whether a novice or a potential top player.

Why not learn to use yourself to your full potential; you know you can do better, so why settle for less?

Plates 51–5. **Exercise 1.** This is a continuous exercise from the forehand to the backhand and back to the forehand, playing against a side wall.

Plate 51. As the ball bounces you must be in the correct position: waiting with your leading foot and racket lined up, and with your wrist back.

Plate 52. Now you have established the link between ball, racket and feet.

A. Use your *wrist* to strike the ball as it descends.
B. Do not forget the follow-through.

Practise this several times.

When you are ready to change to the backhand, you must decide before the ball returns to you from the wall that you will hit it at an angle that will cause it to land on your backhand.

Plate 53. You pivot on your left foot, bringing your racket and right foot round waiting for the ball to bounce. Maintain your position, with your foot in relationship to the bounce of the ball. Line up your racket with the ball.

Plate 54. Your wrist is back and ready to strike.

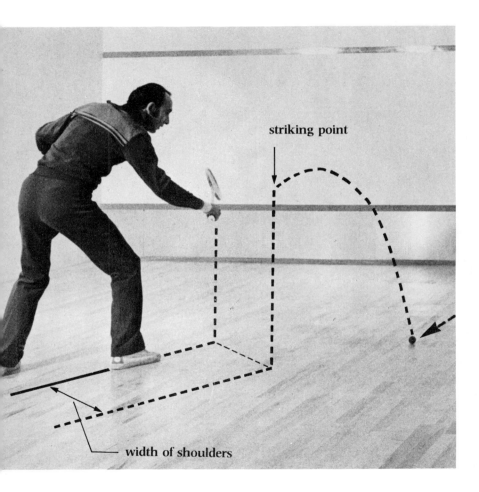

striking point

width of shoulders

Plate 55. Bring your wrist forward, striking the ball on its descent. Do not forget to follow through. Practise this several times.

12 · The missing dimension- your approach to the game __

You have probably realized by now that there are natural laws within the game which have to be obeyed. We must live in harmony with them, and not try to fight them, since they are the basic ingredients of the game. The alternative is to fail, or suffer great frustration.

For example, if you are baking a cake and forget to include one of the basic ingredients, you get no cake. On the other hand, if you follow the recipe faithfully the cake will be successful. So you must never, even subconsciously, become complacent and think you know it all. The moment you ignore the basic principles you will begin to change your game, applying your own method instead of the correct one.

First, it is necessary to prove to ourselves that what we are doing makes sense, and to know, see and feel from the results that it is working. Then we can go on to develop the right effect.

Secondly, always be aware of the existence of the laws and put them into practice.

Thirdly, be aware of yourself and your tendencies and weaknesses within the understanding and the framework of the game. You may not realize that you have them and may need someone else, preferably a coach, to point out the bad points for you. If, as a person, you can understand and accept useful criticism, then you will continue to develop all your life, and not only on a squash court. We all make mistakes — become aware of yourself. Your concentration will improve and your confidence grow. You will develop, and become more proficient at the game. Without this constant development, life becomes dull. There must always be some achievement to look forward to.

In this way your success at squash can be guaranteed. If you follow the correct method from the outset and remain consistently faithful to it, you cannot fail. The good way always gets better and better, the bad way only gets worse.

This, then, is my formula for success.

1. Prove to yourself that the laws of the game exist, and that they work.

2. Be aware of those laws at all times.

3. Be aware of yourself.

4. Reach an understanding of yourself, and of the game.

5. Put it all into practice.

6. Apply yourself single-mindedly.

7. Persevere; never flag in your pursuit of better results.

These principles are part of the laws of success for everyone, in everything.

One more thing I should like to mention before letting you into a secret. Having proved that what I have taught in the earlier pages is correct you will develop confidence, knowing that what you are doing is right. All that you have to do is apply this teaching again and again, until it becomes habitual and is automatic. Any contradictory statements are incorrect, and can only confuse you.

But what is the secret I mentioned? We must take into account the great human potential that we all have; we are unique beings in that we have been given initiative, the initiative that comes from awareness and understanding. It gives us the realization of what is needed to rectify any problem. A human being needs to *know* and to *prove* what is right and what is wrong.

An electronic computer, no matter how marvellous it may be, can only function within the parameters of its programme

— its understanding is totally limited to that programme. It cannot think or rectify mistakes independently, although it can be geared to catch certain errors. It does not have the personal initiative and adaptability of the human mind, which would enable it to execute any action, not just those it is programmed to execute.

But we, always likely to make mistakes, score over the machine in that we have the ability to correct a mistake instantly. But, the point is, we must be aware of right and wrong before we can correct that mistake. I have shown you the right way to enable you to correct your own faults. But never feel that you will reach perfection; rather, remain humble, strive for perfection, and always be willing to learn. Some of the top squash players of the moment are extremely modest men, never considering that they know all there is to know, but always aiming for improvement.

Here is another simple fact: each person has to make his own individual choice to follow the correct route. So do not take it on trust when I say that my way is the right way; go out and prove it for yourself.

On the squash court, as in life, you must accept that you are sharing with someone else. This is especially true when you are a beginner. It is easy to injure your opponent by un- intentionally hitting him with your racket. Winning at all costs is not the most important thing; there is no point in injuring your partner, even if it might mean that you will lose. Instead of trying to win in the shortest possible time, you and your partner could try to keep the ball going continu- ously in a long rally. *Why not try it some time?* It will make a refreshing change from squabbling over points, and I promise you it will be more fun.

I have played squash at international level for twenty years, and it took me ten of those years simply to understand the points that I have given you, however obvious they may seem in retrospect. It took seven more years to discover that there were definite laws within the game. I have tried to put all that knowledge in this book, in a simple form, so make full use of it. Write to me if you feel that you would like to.

Pupil: What are these laws you talk about, Samir? Are they confined to the game of squash, or are they laws within all walks of life?

Samir: The dictionary defines a law as 'A general principle deduced from facts. An invariable sequence of events in nature.' So you see, natural law does not depend on circumstances, it is not man-made. It exists, and all we can do is discover it. It is a part of life and never changes. So, when I refer to a law within the context of squash, I am asking you to tune into something which is there and is unchanging, not something which I made up. A law is a relationship, and unless we maintain that relationship, we are breaking the law and will pay the penalty of failure.

Pupil: How can I tune into these laws and learn to abide by them?

Samir: The first thing is to understand why certain things happen! The second is to go on and prove that they are true, to such an extent that you would be happy to recommend them to others. Knowing the facts and proving them produces the confidence we need. Confidence only comes when we experience something for ourselves, and come to believe in it.

Pupil: Why do I have to prove it for myself before I can believe in it? I've seen you do it dozens of times. Surely that's enough proof?

Samir: No. You may always retain a niggling doubt in the back of your mind that I am able to do it because of the skill gained through many years' experience, even if you aren't aware that you are thinking it! To gain complete certainty, I want you to prove that you can do it too. The laws don't just belong to me, you know, they belong to us all. Everyone can succeed instantly if they can make themselves obey the natural laws.

13 · More about your approach to the game _____

This chapter is about fundamentals.

Your frame of mind ought to be that of sharing, rather than winning. Spending time on a court with a friend or fellow learner, just rallying back and forth, is very enjoyable, and also gives you a chance to improve your strokes in a relaxed situation. Then, at the end of, say, half an hour, you may feel that you want to play a short game, simply for interest's sake, and to put all those shots you have just practised into a competitive situation. This is always a much more pleasant way of learning than, from the beginning, being only interested in beating that particular opponent.

When you begin to feel more competent, and have developed the right kind of courage, I would still advise you to have at least ten minutes' practice before a match, making that match the best of three, or the best of five, as remaining time permits, but never cutting your practice time short.

When you eventually enter a league, or anything on those lines, or if you have a particular friend that you are trying to beat in every match you play, then winning does become important and your attitude must change. My advice to you when entering a competitive situation is always to remain cool. Think before you hit the ball. Try to put into practice all that you have learned. Remember all the fundamentals. By now you should have made the remarkable discovery that the squash ball remains airborne between bounces for far longer than you would think possible, so take your time. Do not rush your shots, thinking that you will be rushing your partner; you will only be rushing yourself. Listen to the music of the ball, it has a sound and a rhythm of its own. The noise it makes when hitting the wall differs according to speed, and allows you to adjust accordingly. Be patient; wait until your partner makes a bad shot through losing his concentration. That is the time to pressurize him, as he will have less time to recover from his stroke and to prepare for yours.

Good shots can be returned with equally good, if not better, shots. A good shot will not always be a winner, whereas an ordinary, or even mediocre, shot can win if your opponent is unprepared. That is why you must wait patiently for the opening which will win the rally.

Be single-minded, concentrating on every stroke. Make sure that they are tight to the wall, that they land in the corner leaving very little bounce, or hardly any room to play. This way, you will force your partner into making an error, with the result that eventually you will score, and tire him out in the process.

Do not try to hit a winner every time, or think that if you hit the ball hard the shot must be a winner. Never relax, assuming that the shot you have played will beat your partner; remember, he may have read the same book!

Be open-minded and easy-going, accepting whatever is best for *both* players, with no inhibitions or restrictions due to vanity. This is the quality of a sportsman.

Always vary your shots. Long shots, 'good-length' shots, shots across court, straight down the wall, drop shots, one at the front and one at the back, etc. In other words, never allow your partner to size you up, or anticipate what you will do next, simply because you are playing the same shot all the time.

Of course, your approach to the game as you walk on to a court will say a great deal about the manner in which you will play, and the way in which you are going to behave. You will be displaying your motives, your relationship to others, and the sort of person you are. I believe one can judge a man's character better by watching him play one game of squash than by spending a lot of time in his company in other circumstances. So read the following carefully, and judge yourself!

Will you accept the referee's decisions, even when the referee is one of your partners just helping out?

Will you accept your opponent's feelings, respecting his opinion when there is a dispute?

Are you out to win at all costs, even if it means hitting him with the ball in the process? Or will you hold back from that stroke, and ask for a let instead?

If you were that player, would you concede the let, and offer it as a penalty point, thanking your partner for not hitting you with the ball?

If, when playing a stroke, your opponent suspects that his ball may have bounced twice, and, although unsure, is willing to concede, do you say 'Let's play it again', or just accept his statement, and gleefully take the point?

If, unseen by your opponent, you hit a ball out of court, would you say nothing and play on, as some do, or point it out to him?

One could go on giving such examples. I am sure you have seen others while watching, or playing, but your reputation as a good sport will mean more to you than any dubious point. And believe me, a bad reputation can spread through a group or club very quickly; bad sportsmen may find it extremely difficult to get partners.

14 · The 'let' controversy _____

I feel very strongly that something needs to be done about the let controversy, and that it would be irresponsible to ignore a situation where there is a lot of confusion. Referees argue among themselves; competition players are confused and disgusted with the standard of refereeing they meet during their travels; the club player too is confused because there is no one to give him a lead.

I give my views on the matter in this chapter, in the hope of triggering a useful discussion.

WHAT CONSTITUTES A LET?

Under the SRA Rule 10, a let is described as 'an undecided stroke, and the service or rally, in respect of which a let is allowed, shall not count, and the server shall serve again from the same box'. This means that if your partner feels that he has been obstructed or that he has not had a fair view of the ball; that if he had played the shot as he had planned he would have hit you with the ball or his racket; or that if he has had to wait to play his shot because of your excessive racket flourishing, etc., then he may ask for a let. He is in fact requesting that the whole rally be played again from the beginning.

A penalty point is requested in those extreme cases where he feels that he could have won the rally with the shot which you obstructed. In other words, he would then win the rally through your fault.

The controversy begins when the offending player disagrees with the call by his partner, or with the referee's eventual decision in the matter.

The main area of disagreement is that covered by Rule 17 – 'Fair view and freedom to play the ball'. Most of this rule is easily understood and applied. The trouble arises when there are different interpretations of the facts. One player feels that he could have reached the ball which had been hidden by his partner, but neither his partner nor the referee agree with him. It is, of course, all a matter of opinion – there is no way that the referee or the other player can prove that, if the appellant had run like mad and taken a swipe at the ball, he would not have been able to return it.

If the player in question has been standing behind his opponent, making it obvious that he could not complete his shot, this makes it easy for the referee to reach the correct decision. Since it is essentially a matter of opinion, it is up to each player to endeavour to show the referee and his opponent that he could have got there had he not been obstructed. This is why you should *always* try to reach the ball.

Unfortunately, when players walk on to a court presided over by a strange referee, they have no way of knowing how he views the let rule. It may take up to three games before they realize what is expected of them. (Some knowledgeable players will take unfair advantage of a player who is less experienced and unaware of the conduct expected by a referee.) In fact, until the players settle down, see which way the wind blows, and establish a relationship, good or bad, with the referee, there is no certainty of how the referee will react. This is a very unsatisfactory situation. The referee is the policeman of the squash court, and he should be completely unbiased and trustworthy.

What is needed is a simple, easily interpreted ruling such as the rule of the road – if we drive on the wrong side we know we are in the wrong and accept any penalty which may be awarded against us. The present situation in squash, however, is more like the free-for-all that used to exist on roundabouts before the 'priority to the right' rule was introduced.

Obviously discussion is needed at every level. Seminars could be arranged; literature could be sent to all international players, referees, and clubs; meetings could be held during big tournaments, when all the top players are in attendance. Once a standard of behaviour is established among the higher echelons of squash, it will quickly percolate down to club level and the grass roots of the sport.

I recently had a conversation with an international player on this very subject and, after I had talked to him for a while on the value of gentlemanly behaviour on court and conceding gracefully when you had made an error, he said, 'But if I behaved in the manner which you advocate, other players would walk all over me and take me for a fool. Other players don't play by the same rules.' I replied 'You are being short-sighted. By using the approach I suggest you will gain two advantages. One, you will remain cool and retain your concentration at all times, and, two, it will always be pleasant to play you. Don't you feel you could convert by example? After all, the whole world looks to you for a lead.' But I don't think I convinced him. The aggression is too ingrained.

I am reminded of a cartoon I once saw, of a normal unassuming type of man getting behind the wheel of a car and turning into a demon. One often sees that happen on a squash court, too. Many players seem to think that all's fair in love and squash, and for forty minutes or so all barriers of social conduct are down. The game undoubtedly tends to heighten the aggression which resides in us all.

SOME HYPOTHETICAL SITUATIONS

A player may play a middle-height ball which comes straight back at him. Realizing his error, and that his partner is behind him, he ducks down at his partner's feet to allow him to play the ball. Despite his efforts, he has unbalanced his partner, who should refrain from playing and claim a point.

Unfortunately, some players feel that whenever they have their opponent at a disadvantage they must attempt a winning shot. If their shot fails, perhaps because they were unbalanced, they should not be able to claim a let. They have played the shot and therefore lost the right to claim. Nevertheless, they frequently do claim, and if they are good actors may well gain the advantage. But had they withheld their shot, they could have claimed a point anyway.

I must point out here that it is, in any case, very dangerous to be caught within the area of your returning ball. When your partner comes to play his stroke, his racket could well injure you in the heat of the game. Because he can see the danger, he will have to slow down and probably change his mind about the type of shot he can play. You will have distracted him, and it is therefore up to you to offer him a point. If he is equally sporting, he will settle for a let.

If a player appears to be slow, and constantly delays moving out of the way, the referee should warn him that points will be awarded against him. This is particularly important when it happens at the back of the court, because the opponent has less chance from this position of playing an outright winner, and the referee can normally only award a let. To abide by the rules, a player must make every effort to move out of his opponent's way, and it is up to the referee to request that he speed up his movements, if necessary. The player must then do so, *and be seen to be doing so*.

When calculating the room a player needs to play his shot, remember that he must approach the ball from the side, allowing room for the bounce. It is your duty, therefore, to grant him that line of approach, since depriving him of it may cause him to finish up too close to the ball. (Refer to Chapter 9 for correct striking positions.) Beginners tend to run straight at the ball rather than to the side of it, but practised players will, if allowed, always adopt the correct method of approach.

POINTS TO BE CONSIDERED WHEN DECIDING BETWEEN A LET AND A PENALTY POINT

In the situation illustrated in figure 29 a penalty point was awarded. Why?

Striker A plays a drop shot, and fails to move immediately the ball leaves his racket. He remains in position a fraction of a second too long. His partner B is coming fast. In a panic, A moves to the left in order to give B room, and a fair view of the ball, consequently placing himself out of position, trapped against the wall.

If B played his shot across court, instead of withholding it because A was obstructing him, it would undoubtedly be a winner, in which case he would score a point. Therefore, he must be awarded the rally.

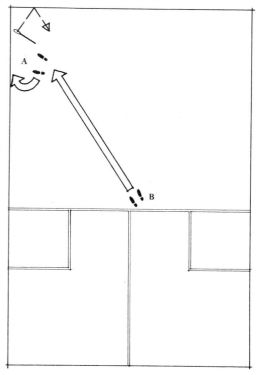

Figure 29.
A penalty point awarded.

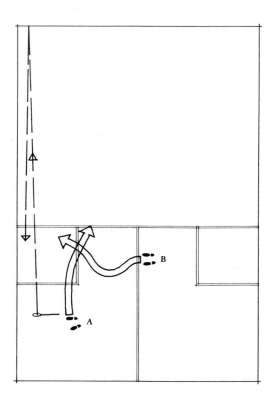

Figure 30.
A let awarded.

Figure 30 illustrates a case where the referee ought to award a let.

Striker A plays a shot down the nearside wall and moves up court without waiting to see what his opponent B will do. He has assumed that B will take the ball after it has bounced simply because that is what he would do himself. But after a slight hesitation B decides to volley the ball, and finds that he is obstructed because A is in his path. Now, A has made every effort to get out of his opponent's way, even if he was a bit premature in assuming where B would play the ball. And B's indecision has been noticed by the referee. On this occasion, the referee would probably decide that it had been six of one and half a dozen of the other, or that B had got himself into trouble, but whichever it was, would have to award a let.

As far as beginners are concerned, it would probably be better if all cases of 'Fair view and freedom to play the ball' were covered by a let, until such time that they both felt that they were quick enough on their feet and capable of controlling the ball. Perhaps they could then agree to call for penalty points; losing a few rallies in this manner is an excellent incentive to speed up your movements and give consideration to your partner's needs.

15 · About clubs and ladders __

If you are not already a member of a squash club you may find that you have a considerable wait ahead of you, as prospective numbers are growing faster than courts can be built. Possibly one of the leisure centres which are springing up in many areas will answer your more immediate needs. In many cases leisure centres offer more opportunities to younger players and are generally cheaper and easier to join.

There are some clubs with long waiting-lists for full membership who will offer daytime-only membership at a somewhat reduced price. If this facility is not available at your local club, why not get in touch with a committee member and suggest that he try this system. The club will probably welcome a chance to utilize empty courts, and thereby increase their revenue.

When joining a club, check that you will be able to receive coaching and that you will be introduced to other players of a similar standard.

Whichever type of club you choose, there is bound to be a league or ladder system which, eventually, you will wish to join. Joining the league will mean that you will always be able to get a game. It also means that you will have the opportunity of playing others of a higher standard than yourself. This will add greatly to your enjoyment and also improve your game. Always remain courteous and, when playing a league or ladder match, reject the pressure to win at all costs.

When knocking up always give your partner a fair share

of the ball; he is entitled to hit the ball as many times as you are. Half-way through knocking-up time, you should swop sides. This gives both players equal time for backhand and forehand practice. It is probably best to maintain a low profile during knocking up. Showing your opponent all your fancy shots may scare him out of winning, but it could equally give him an insight into your game which you would rather he did not have. Be warned!

Unless your standard of play is well known to the club – if, for instance, you have already beaten some league members – then you may have to start right at the very bottom when you enter the leagues. Do not worry – you will soon find your own level. Most clubs follow the same system: approximately five players per league and a set time in which to play your four games. Promotion and relegation depend on the results.

The ladder differs in that all participants are listed on one board, and all are open to challenges. The idea is to challenge someone who is higher than you in the ladder and, upon winning, taking the position immediately above theirs. The rules vary from club to club, and in some cases you may have to beat that player twice before supplanting him; in others, only once.

If you have the time, you may wish to enter both league and ladder, but this can be time-consuming and gruelling. I would suggest that those who have plenty of time join the league, where there is a time limit on games. Those with a little less time may find that the ladder is more suitable as, in most cases, there is no time limit. You should remember, however, that if you are challenged and cannot play within a certain time you may lose your place to the challenger without even stepping on court.

It is unfortunate that in most cases ladders stagnate or die as, eventually, everyone settles into their natural positions; the top five or ten players will probably play for the club team and be impossible to dislodge. Nevertheless, it is a good method of beginning club life and of meeting new people.

16 · Blueprint for success ____

This book is for everybody, not just the champions! Champions will always be champions, although they too could improve by applying these laws. But the aim of this book is to enable *you* to enjoy yourself to the best of your potential.

What I am saying in this book is summed up in plates 56 and 57. This is the blueprint for an unruffled, relaxed and, above all, confident squash player.

Plate 56. **The gear and the clutch**

In conclusion: Every time you are making a stroke, whether it is forehand or backhand, you must get the clutch, (your foot) and the gear (your racket) into relationship with the ball.

The racket as
the gear

The foot as
the clutch

Plate 57. **The accelerator**

These must be linked mentally with the striking point before you can use the accelerator (your wrist). You use your wrist by taking it back and then forward in a plane parallel to the floor and related to the height of the ball.

The wrist as accelerator

Appendix

THE RULES OF THE SINGLES GAME OF SQUASH RACKETS

Approved by the International Squash Rackets Federation (ISRF) to be effective from 1 January 1977.* (These rules refer to the game of Squash Rackets in respect of the game as played on courts, the specifications for which were first determined by The Squash Rackets Association (Great Britain).

1. THE GAME, HOW PLAYED. The game of Squash Rackets is played between two players with standard rackets, with balls officially approved by ISRF and in a rectangular court of standard dimensions, enclosed on all four sides.

2. THE SCORE. A match shall consist of the best of three or five games at the option of the promoters of the competition. Each game is 9 points up; that is to say, the player who first wins 9 points wins the game, except that, on the score being called 8 all for the first time, Hand-out may choose, before the next service is delivered, to continue the game to 10, in which case the player who first scores two more points wins the game. Hand-out must in either case clearly indicate his choice to the Marker, if any, and to his opponent.

Note to Referees. If Hand-out does not make clear his choice before the next service, the Referee shall stop play and require him to do so.

3. POINTS, HOW SCORED. Points can only be scored by Hand-in. When a player fails to serve or to make a good return in accordance with the rules, the opponent wins the stroke. When Hand-in wins a stroke, he scores a point; when Hand-out wins a stroke, he becomes Hand-in.

4. THE RIGHT TO SERVE. The right to serve first is decided by the spin of a racket. Thereafter the server continues to serve until he loses a stroke, when his opponent becomes the server, and so on throughout the match.

5. SERVICE. The ball before being struck shall be dropped or thrown in the air and shall not touch the walls or floor. The ball shall be served direct on to the front wall, so that on its return, unless volleyed, it would fall to the floor within the back quarter of the court opposite to the server's box from which the service has been delivered.

At the beginning of each game and of each hand, the server may serve from either box, but after scoring a point he shall then serve from the other, and so on alternately as long as he remains Hand-in or until the end of the game. If the server serves from

*With amendments as of June 1978.

the wrong box, there shall be no penalty and the service shall count as if served from the correct box, except that Hand-out may, if he does not attempt to take the service, demand that it be served from the other box.

A player with the use of only one arm may utilize his racket to project the ball into the air.

6. GOOD SERVICE. A service is good which is not a fault or which does not result in the server serving his hand-out in accordance with Rule 9. If the server serves one fault, he shall serve again.

7. FAULT. A service is a fault (unless the server serves his hand-out under Rule 9):

(a) If the server fails to stand with at least one foot on the floor within, and not touching the line surrounding the service box at the moment of striking the ball (called a foot fault).

(b) If the ball is served on to, or below, the cut line.

(c) If the ball served first touches the floor on, or in front of, the short line, or on or outside that half court line.

8. FAULT, IF TAKEN. Hand-out may take a fault. If he attempts to do so, the service thereupon becomes good and the ball continues in play. If he does not attempt to do so, the ball shall cease to be in play, provided that, if the ball, before it bounces twice upon the floor, touches the server or anything he wears or carries, the server shall lose the stroke.

9. SERVING HAND-OUT. The server serves his hand-out and loses the stroke:

(a) If the ball is served on to, or below, the board, or out, or against any part of the court before the front wall;

(b) If the ball is not dropped or thrown in the air, or touches the wall or floor before being struck, or if he fails to strike the ball, or strikes it more than once;

(c) If he serves two consecutive faults;

(d) If the ball, before it has bounced twice upon the floor, or has been struck by his opponent, touches the server or anything he wears or carries.

10. LET. A let is an undecided stroke, and the service or rally, in respect of which a let is allowed, shall not count and the server shall serve again from the same box. A let shall not annul a previous fault.

Note to Referees.
This last sentence applies only to a second or subsequent service after a fault has not been taken.

11. THE PLAY. After a good service has been delivered, the players return the ball alternately until one or other fails to make a good return, or the ball otherwise ceases to be in play in accordance with the rules.

12. GOOD RETURN. A return is good if the ball, before it has bounced twice upon the floor is returned by the striker on to the front wall above the board, without touching the floor or any part of the striker's body or clothing, provided the ball is not hit twice or out.

Note to Referees.
It shall not be considered a good return if the ball touches the board before or after it hits the front wall.

13. STROKES, HOW WON. A player wins a stroke:

(a) Under Rule 9;

(b) If the opponent fails to make a good return of the ball in play;

(c) If the ball in play touches his opponent or anything he wears or carries, except as is otherwise provided by Rules 14 and 15.

(d) If a stroke is awarded by the Referee as provided for in the Rules.

14.   HITTING AN OPPONENT WITH THE BALL. If an otherwise good return of the ball has been made, but before reaching the front wall it hits the striker's opponent, or his racket, or anything he wears or carries, then:

(a) If the ball would have made a good return, and would have struck the front wall without first touching any other wall, the striker shall win the stroke, except if the striker shall have followed the ball round, and so turned, before playing the ball, a let shall be allowed.

(b) If the ball would otherwise have made a good return, a let shall be allowed unless in the Referee's opinion, a winning stroke has been intercepted: then the striker shall win the stroke.

(c) If the ball would not have made a good return, the striker shall lose the stroke.

The ball shall cease to be in play, even if it subsequently goes up.

15.   FURTHER ATTEMPTS TO HIT THE BALL. If the striker strikes at, and misses the ball, he may make further attempts to return it. If, after being missed, the ball touches his opponent, or his racket, or anything he wears or carries, then:

(a) If the striker would otherwise have made a good return, a let shall be allowed.

(b) If the striker could not have made a good return, he loses the stroke.

If any such further attempt is successful, but the ball, before reaching the front wall, hits the striker's opponent, or his racket, or anything he wears or carries, a let shall be allowed, and Rule 14(a) shall not apply.

16.   APPEALS.

(a) An appeal may be made against any decision of the Marker, except for (b) (i) below.

(b)   (i) No appeal shall be made in respect of the Marker's call of 'foot fault' or 'fault' to the first service.

(ii) If the Marker calls 'foot fault' or 'fault' to the second service, the server may appeal, and if the decision is reversed, a let shall be allowed.

(iii) If the Marker allows the second service, Hand-out may appeal, either immediately, or at the end of the rally, if he has played the ball, and if the decision is reversed, Hand-in becomes Hand-out.

(iv) If the Marker does not call 'foot fault' or 'fault' to the first service, Hand-out may appeal that the service was a foot fault or fault, provided he makes no attempt to play the ball. If the Marker does not call 'Out' or 'Not up' to the first service, Hand-out may appeal, either immediately or at the end of the rally, if he has played the ball. In either case, if the appeal is dis-allowed, Hand-out shall lose the stroke.

(c) An appeal under Rule 12 shall be made at the end of the rally.

(d) In all cases where a let is desired, an appeal shall be made to the Referee with the words 'Let, please'. Play shall thereupon cease until the Referee has given his decision.

(e) No appeal may be made after the delivery of a service for anything that occurred before that service was delivered.

17.   FAIR VIEW AND FREEDOM TO PLAY THE BALL.

(a) After playing a ball, a player must make every effort to get out of his opponent's way. That is:

(i) A player must make every effort to give his opponent a fair view of the ball, so that he may sight it adequately for the purpose of playing it.

(ii) A player must make every effort not to interfere with, or crowd, his opponent in the latter's attempt to get to, or play, the ball.

(iii) A player must make every effort to allow his opponent, as far as the latter's position permits, freedom to play the ball directly to the front wall, or side walls near the front wall.

(b) If any such form of interference has occurred, and, in the opinion of the Referee, the player has not made every effort to avoid causing it, the Referee shall on appeal, or stopping play without waiting for an appeal, award the stroke to his opponent.

(c) However, if interference has occurred, but in the opinion of the Referee the player has made every effort to avoid causing it, the Referee shall on appeal, or stopping play without waiting for an appeal, award a let, except that if his opponent is prevented from making a winning return by such interference or by distraction from the player, the Referee shall award the stroke to the opponent.

(d) When, in the opinion of the Referee, a player refrains from playing the ball, which, if played, would clearly and undoubtedly have won the rally under the terms of Rule 14(a) or (b), he shall be awarded the stroke.

Note to Referees.
(i) The practice of impeding an opponent in his efforts to play the ball by crowding or obscuring his view, is highly detrimental to the game, and Referees should have no hesitation in enforcing paragraph (b) above.
(ii) The words 'interfere with' in (a)(ii) above must be interpreted to include the case of a player having to wait for an excessive swing of his opponent's racket.

18. LET, WHEN ALLOWED. Notwithstanding anything contained in these rules, and provided always that the striker could have made a good return:

(a) A let may be allowed:
(i) If, owing to the position of the striker, his opponent is unable to avoid being touched by the ball before the return is made.

Notes to Referees.
This rule shall be construed to include the cases of the striker, whose position in front of his opponent makes it impossible for the latter to see the ball, or who shapes as if to play the ball and changes his mind at the last moment, preferring to take the ball off the back wall, the ball in either case hitting his opponent, who is between the striker and the back wall. This is not, however, to be taken as conflicting in any way with the Referee's duties under Rule 17.
(ii) If the ball in play touches any articles lying in the court.
(iii) If the striker refrains from hitting the ball owing to a reasonable fear of injuring his opponent.
(iv) If the striker, in the act of playing the ball, touches his opponent.
(v) If the Referee is asked to decide an appeal and is unable to do so.
(vi) If a player drops his racket, calls out or in any other way distracts his opponent, and the Referee considers that such occurrence has caused the opponent to lose the stroke.

(b) A let shall be allowed:
(i) If Hand-out is not ready, and does not attempt to take the service.
(ii) If a ball breaks during play.
(iii) If an otherwise good return has been made, but the ball goes out of court on its first bounce.
(iv) As provided for in Rules 14, 15, 16(b)(iii), 23 and 24.

(c) No let shall be allowed if the player makes an attempt to play the ball except as provided for under Rules 15, 18(a)(iv), 18(b)(ii) and 18(b)(iii).

(d) Unless an appeal is made by one of the players, no let shall be allowed except where these rules definitely provide for a let, namely, Rules 14(a) and (b), 17 and 18(b)(ii) and (iii).

19. NEW BALL. At any time, when the ball is not in actual play, a new ball may be substituted by mutual consent of the players, or, on appeal by either player, at the discretion of the Referee.

20. KNOCK-UP.

(a) The Referee shall allow on the court of play a period not exceeding five minutes to the two players together for the purpose of knocking up, or in the event of the players electing to knock-up separately, the Referee shall allow the first player a period of three and a half minutes and to his opponent, two and a half minutes.

(b) Where a new ball has been substituted under Rule 18(b)(ii) or 19, the Referee shall allow the ball to be knocked-up to playing condition. Play shall resume on the direction of the Referee, or prior mutual consent of the players.

(c) Between games the ball shall remain on the floor of the court in view and knocking-up shall not be permitted except by mutual consent of the players.

21. PLAY IN A MATCH IS TO BE CONTINUOUS. After the first service is delivered, play shall be continuous so far as is practical, provided that:

(a) At any time play may be suspended owing to bad light or other circumstances beyond the control of the players, for such period as the Referee shall decide. In the event of play being suspended for the day, the match shall start afresh, unless both players agree to the contrary.

(b) The Referee shall award a game to the opponent of any player, who, in his opinion persists, after due warning, in delaying the play in order to recover his strength or wind, or for any other reason.

(c) An interval of one minute shall be permitted between games and of two minutes between the fourth and fifth games of a five-game match. A player may leave the court during such intervals, but shall be ready to resume play at the end of the stated time. When ten seconds of the interval permitted between games are left, the Marker shall call 'Ten seconds' to warn the players to be ready to resume play. Should either player fail to do so when required by the Referee, a game may be awarded to his opponent.

(d) In the event of an injury, the Referee may require a player to continue play or concede the match, except where the injury is contributed to by his opponent, or where it was caused by dangerous play on the part of the opponent. In the former case, the Referee may allow time for the injured player to receive attention and recover, and in the latter, the injured player shall be awarded the match under Rule 24(c)(ii).

(e) In the event of a ball breaking, a new ball may be knocked-up, as provided for in Rule 20(b).

Notes to Referees.

(i) In allowing time for a player to receive attention and recover, the Referee should ensure that there is no conflict with the obligation of a player to comply with Rule 21(b), that is, that the effects of the injury are not exaggerated and used as an excuse to recover strength and wind.

(ii) The Referee should not interpret the words 'contributed to' by the opponent to include the situation where the injury to the player is a result of that player occupying an unnecessarily close position to his opponent.

22. CONTROL OF A MATCH. A match is normally controlled by a Referee, assisted by a Marker. One person may be appointed to carry out the functions of both Referee and Marker. When a decision has been made by a Referee, he shall announce it to the players and the Marker shall repeat it with the subsequent score.

Up to one hour before the commencement of a match either player may request a Referee and/or a Marker other than appointed, and this request may be considered and a substitute appointed. Players are not permitted to request any such change after the commencement of a match, unless both agree to do so. In either case the decision as to whether an official is to be replaced or not must remain in the hands of the Tournament Referee, where applicable.

23. DUTIES OF MARKER.

(a) The Marker calls the play and the score, with the server's score first. He shall call 'Foot Fault'; 'Fault'; 'Out or 'Not up' or 'Down' as appropriate.

(b) If in the course of play the Marker calls 'Not up' or 'Out' or in the case of a second service 'Fault' or 'Foot fault' then the rally shall cease.

(c) If the Marker's decision is reversed on appeal, a let shall be allowed, except as provided for in Rule 24(b)(iv) and (v).

(d) Any service or return shall be considered good unless otherwise called.

(e) After the server has served a fault, which has not been taken, the Marker shall repeat the score and add the words 'One fault', before the server serves again. This call should be repeated should subsequent rallies end in a let, until the point is finally decided.

(f) When no Referee is appointed, the Marker shall exercise all the powers of the Referee.

(g) If the Marker is unsighted or uncertain, he shall call on the Referee to make the relevant decision; if the latter is unable to do so, a let shall be allowed.

24. DUTIES OF REFEREE.

(a) The Referee shall award Lets and Strokes and make decisions where called for by the rules, and shall decide all appeals, including those against the Marker's calls and decisions. The decision of the Referee shall be final.

(b) He shall in no way intervene in the Marker's calling except:
    (i) Upon appeal by one of the players.
    (ii) As provided for in Rule 17.
    (iii) When it is evident that the score has been incorrectly called, in which case he should draw the Marker's attention to the fact.
    (iv) When the Marker has failed to call the ball 'Not up' or 'Out' and on appeal he rules that such was in fact the case, the stroke should be awarded accordingly.
    (v) When the Marker has called 'Not up' or 'Out' and on appeal he rules that this was not the case, a Let shall be allowed except that if in the Referee's opinion, the Marker's call had interrupted an undoubted winning return, he shall award the stroke accordingly.
    (vi) In exceptional circumstances when he is absolutely convinced that the Marker has made an obvious error in stopping play or allowing play to continue, he shall immediately rule accordingly.

(c) The Referee is responsible that all times laid down in the rules are strictly adhered to.

(d) In exceptional cases, the Referee may order:
    (i) A player, who has left the court, to play on.
    (ii) A player to leave the court and to award the match to the opponent.
    (iii) A match to be awarded to a player whose opponent fails to be present in court within ten minutes of the advertised time of play.
    (iv) Play to be stopped in order to warn that the conduct of one or both of the players is leading to an infringement of the rules. A Referee should avail himself of this rule as early as possible when either player is showing a tendency to break the provisions of Rule 17.

(e) If after a warning a player continues to contravene Rule 20(c) the Referee shall award a game to the opponent.

25. COLOUR OF PLAYERS' CLOTHING.

For amateur events under the control of the ISRF, players are required to wear all white clothing, provided however, the ISRF officers at their sole discretion can waive compliance with this rule.

Member countries of the ISRF may legislate, if they so desire, to allow clothing of a light pastel colour to be worn for all other events under their control.

The Referee's decision thereon is final.

Note: Footwear is deemed clothing for this rule.

DEFINITIONS

Board or Tin. The expression denoting a band, the top edge of which is 483mm (19 inches) from the floor across the lower part of the front wall above which the ball must be returned before the stroke is good.

Cut Line. A line upon the front wall, the top edge of which is 1·829m (6 feet) above the floor and extending the full width of the court.

Down. The expression used to indicate that a ball has been struck against the tin or board.

Game Ball. The state of the game when the server requires one point to win is said to be 'Game Ball'.

Half-Court Line. A line set out upon the floor parallel to the side walls, dividing the back half of the court into two equal parts.

Hand-in. The player who serves.

Hand-out. The player who receives the service; also the expression used to indicate that Hand-in has become Hand-out.

Hand. The period from the time when a player becomes Hand-in until he becomes Hand-out.

Match Ball. The state of the match when the server requires one point to win is said to be Match Ball.

Not-up. The expression used to denote that a ball has not been served or returned above the board in accordance with the rules.

Out. The ball is out when it touches the front, sides or back of the court above the area prepared for play or passes over any cross bars or other part of the roof of the court. The lines delimiting such area, the lighting equipment and the roof are out.

Point. A point is won by the player who is Hand-in and who wins a stroke.

Quarter Court. One part of the back half of the court which has been divided into two equal parts by the half-court line.

Service Box or Box. A delimited area in each quarter court from within which Hand-in serves.

Short Line. A line set out upon the floor parallel to and 5·486m (18 feet) from the front wall and extending the full width of the court.

Stop. Expression used by the Referee to stop play.

Striker. The player whose turn it is to play after the ball has hit the front wall.

Stroke. A stroke is won by the player whose opponent fails to serve or make a good return in accordance with the rules.

Time. Expression used by the Referee to start play.

APPENDIX II

DIMENSIONS OF A SINGLES COURT

Length: 9·75m (32 feet). Breadth: 6·40m (21 feet)

Height to upper edge of cut line on front wall	..	..	..	1·83m (6 feet)
Height to lower edge of front-wall line	..	..	..	4·57m (15 feet)
Height to lower edge of back-wall line	..	..	..	2·13m (7 feet)

Appendix: The rules of squash   171

Distance to further edge of short line from front wall ..   ..   5·49m (18 feet)
Height to upper edge of board from ground   ..   ..   ..   0·48m (19 inches)
Thickness of board (flat or rounded at top): 12·5mm to 25mm ($\frac{1}{2}$ to 1 inch)
Height of side-wall: The diagonal line joining the front-wall and the back-wall lines.

The service boxes shall be entirely enclosed on three sides within the court by lines, the short line forming the side nearest to the front wall, the side wall bounding the fourth side.

The internal dimensions of the service boxes shall be 1·601m (5ft 3in.).

All dimensions in the court shall be measured, where practicable, from the junction of the floor and front wall.

All lines marking the boundaries of the court shall be 50mm (2 inches) in width and all other lines shall not exceed 50mm (2 inches) in width. All lines shall be coloured red. In respect of the outer boundary lines on the walls, it is suggested that the plaster should be so shaped as to produce a concave channel along such lines.

APPENDIX III

DIMENSIONS OF A RACKET

The overall length shall not exceed 685mm (27 inches). The internal stringing area shall not exceed 215mm ($8\frac{1}{2}$ inches) in length by 184mm ($7\frac{1}{4}$ inches) in breadth and the framework of the head shall measure not more than 14mm (9/16 inch) across the face by 20mm (13/16 inch) deep.

The framework of the head shall be of wood. The handle shaft shall be made of wood, cane, metal or glass fibre. The grip and foundation may be made of any suitable material.

APPENDIX IV

SPECIFICATION FOR SQUASH RACKET BALLS

The ball must conform to the following:

1. It must weigh not less than 23·3 grammes and not more than 24·6 grammes (approximately 360-380 grains).
2. Its diameter must be not less than 39·5mm and not more than 41·5mm (approximately 1·56 to 1·63 inches).
3. It must have a surface finish which guarantees continuing correct rebound.
4. It must be of a type specifically approved for championship play by the International Squash Rackets Federation.
5. Compression Specification:
   (i) The ball is mounted in an apparatus and a load of 0·5 kgm is applied which deforms the ball slightly. Subsequent deformation in the test is measured from this datum.
   (ii) An additional load of 2·4 kgm is applied and this deforms the ball further. The deformation from the datum position is recorded.
   (iii) The deformation obtained in (ii) should be between 3 and 7mm for balls of playing properties acceptable to the ISRF.

APPENDIX V

CONSTRUCTION OF A COURT
(INTERNATIONAL CHAMPIONSHIP STANDARD)

The front wall should be constructed of concrete, brick or similar material with a near smooth concrete or plaster finish. The side and rear walls to be constructed of similar materials. The rear wall, for viewing purposes, can be constructed of glass or similar materials.

All walls shall be white or near white. The board shall be white or near white in colour and made of some resonant material. The top edge shall be either rounded or flat incorporating a red line to a depth of 50mm (2 inches) measured from the top.

The floor shall be constructed of light coloured wooden boards which will run length-wise and not across the court. The floor must be level (horizontal).

The area above the height of play on the back wall (if wall continues upwards) should be constructed of some resonant material.

All lines **shall** be coloured red.

The minimum clear height above the front wall playing surface to be 1·25 metres, giving a clear height from the court floor of 5·8 metres (19 feet).

The minimum clear height at 3·5 metres back from the front wall to be 6·4 metres above the floor (21 feet).

Where a flat ceiling is used the height set at 3·5 metres back should apply as a minimum.

The ceiling should be white or near white.

NOTES TO PLAYERS AND OFFICIALS

Incorporating ISRF Rule Changes, in which basically the aim has been to tidy up the previous rules, make life easier for Referees by giving penalties they can award rather than extreme measures they are reluctant to impose, clarify the wording of some rules and in general work towards a code which can be interpreted consistently by officials in all member nations of the ISRF.

In order to assist players in understanding the correct application of the rules regarding marking and refereeing the following points are set out:

1. **Under Rule 22:** DUTIES OF A MARKER. It is clearly stated that the control of the game is vested in the marker and it is his duty to call the play and the score.

2. **Under Rule 23:** THE REFEREE. A referee may be appointed **to whom all appeals shall be directed** including appeals against the marker's decisions and calls.

A referee may not normally interfere with the marker's counting of the game **except upon appeal** by one of the players, unless he is completely certain that the Marker has made an error in the calling of the score.

The exception to this is the provision of **Rule 17:** FAIR VIEW, where the referee may interpose a let or award a stroke if he considers that circumstances warrant such. In general no let shall be allowed unless an appeal is made by one of the players (see Rule 18).

In connection with the above it is stressed that markers and referees have been encouraged to enforce the provisions of Rule 17 bearing in mind that it is '**unnecessary obstruction**' which is penalized **irrespective of whether it is intentional** or not.

3. It is pointed out that where a marker only is in attendance he exercises all the powers of a referee and it is therefore considered to be in order for a player to direct an appeal to him **as referee** from any decision or calls made by him in his capacity **as marker**.

4. Anything in the nature of aggressive or temperamental appealing will not be tolerated by the SRA.

5. By noting these points it is hoped, NOT that players will habitually resort to indiscriminate appealing, but that they will achieve a better understanding of how to play to a referee.

NOTES TO ALL MARKERS AND REFEREES IN THE OPEN CHAMPIONSHIP

The SRA is particularly anxious that the standard of Refereeing and Marking should be as high as possible, and that decisions should be consistent. With this in mind, it is hoped that all officials will make a most thorough study of the rules so that they may be able to cope authoritatively and promptly with any situation that may arise. It is also hoped that greater consistency may be achieved over the granting or refusal of lets and the award of points, and Referees are asked to study the following points, which are intended to guide them in their interpretations of the Rules.

LETS
Basically a let shall be allowed when a rally ceases because the striker has been accidentally impeded by his opponent from seeing or striking the ball in any direction he wishes. However, even if the striker were **accidentally** prevented from attempting a shot, which, in the Referee's opinion, would have been a winner, this incoming striker shall be awarded the rally.

CLAIMING LETS
If necessary, players should be reminded of the correct method of claiming a let, as laid down in Rule 16(iii), and in the absence of a verbal request the Marker should call the score in accordance with the outcome of the rally.

A let should be refused if the striker could not, in the Referee's opinion have made a good return in any event.

BARGING AND DANGEROUS RACKET SWING
When a player appeals for a let, he must have demonstrated conclusively by his movements immediately prior to the appeal that he could have retrieved the ball.

This does not mean he should barge his opponent. Should he do so, the Referee should immediately warn him that such action could lead to disqualification through injury to his opponent. Excessive and dangerous swinging of the racket should be treated in the same way.

POINTS—WHEN AWARDED
The award of a point should be made automatically for any form of deliberate obstruction, and also in certain cases of accidental obstruction. 'Deliberate' obstruction must be taken to mean not only a deliberate attempt to move into the opponent's way, **but also the lack of deliberate effort to move out of it. Rule 17 demands a positive action on the part of each player to move clear after playing a stroke,** and any failure to do this must result in the award of a point to the opponent, regardless of whether the latter was in a position to attempt a winner.

For the award of a point in cases of accidental obstruction, the impeded player must have been prevented from attempting a winning stroke. The four main situations when this occurs are:

(a) If a player has just retrieved the ball in the front of the court, but is off balance, unable to move clear of his own shot and his body thus prevents his opponent from hitting a winner past him.

(b) If a player in the back of the court has played a poor shot which has returned towards himself, and he fails to give room to his opponent to attempt a winner in the front of the court.

(c) If a player close to a side wall has hit the ball inaccurately so that it returns on a line between himself and the centre of the court, and he endeavours to regain the centre of the court by moving across the line of the ball, and in so doing prevents his opponent from having a fair view and unimpeded stroke.

(d) If a player refrains from playing his stroke for fear of hitting his opponent with the ball, and it was obvious that, had he gone through with the shot, it would have been a winner, as his opponent was directly between him and the front wall. The reasoning behind this is that a ruthless player will win the point in this situation by hitting the ball into his opponent, and it is unfair to penalize a pleasant player.

EARLY RALLIES

In the early stages of a match both players will be either consciously or unconsciously assessing the Referee's interpretation of the rules of obstruction. On no account should a Referee award a let when the situation demands the award of a point **solely because the match has only just started.** Similarly, a Referee must not feel reluctant to award a point at match point if the situation demands it.

WARNING PLAYERS

The Referee is perfectly within his rights to call either or both players over at any time in the match—and even to stop a rally for the purpose—in order to issue a warning that they are in danger of infringing a rule and may in future be penalized.

DANGEROUS RACKET SWING

It was necessary in a recent season to issue a very severe warning to all championship players that dangerous swinging of the racket would not be permitted. If a Referee feels that a player is endangering his opponent by an exaggerated racket swing he should warn him and thereafter is completely within his rights to disqualify him if the warning. is not heeded. Attention is also drawn to Rule 21, so that Referees need not make too hasty a decision, if a player is injured during the course of a match. In such circumstances a Referee may well wish to suspend temporarily and announce his decision on the award of the match, one way or the other, or its replay, after further consideration of the injury itself and its cause.

UNEXPECTED REBOUND OF BALL

When a ball jumps out from a front corner unexpectedly, causing interference, a point shall be awarded if the incoming striker could, in the Referee's opinion have played a winner. **If, however, the incoming striker is as surprised as his opponent** and not sufficiently poised to execute this winner, a let shall be given.

PLAYER WRONG-FOOTED

Another source of interpretation trouble. If a player is wrong-footed, i.e. he anticipates his opponent hitting the ball one way, starts moving that way, but has guessed wrong, then changes direction to find his opponent in the way, he should only be given a 'let' on appeal if he has recovered so as to show conclusively that he could have made a good return.

TIME WASTING

Referees are also asked to keep a strict eye on time wasting, both during the actual game and the intervals between games.

Rule 21 now allows a referee to award a game rather than the whole match and enables a referee to penalize time wasting etc. in a way he will feel able to do. The interval between games shall begin from the moment the Referee awards the game.

Rule 21(b) allows the referee to award the game in progress if a player persists in delaying play after due warning.

Under Rule 21(c), the call of '10 seconds' is now obligatory and gives the players no excuse for not being ready, so the referee can feel easy in his mind about awarding a game if one of the players is not ready.

INJURY

It was accepted that there are three types of injury or sickness that might arise in play and be dealt with somewhat differently:

(a) Self-inflicted injury, sickness or exhaustion on court; players should continue playing or concede. However discretion should be used both in allowing a player to leave court should he ask, and also in the time allowed in which he may recover himself. Only a few moments may be permitted for the player to recover and play on.

(b) Opponent solely to blame; in which case play was dangerous and the opponent should be disqualified. The referee only can determine what happened in deciding this action.

(c) Caused through fault or action of both players; in minor cases a player may be given a minute in which to recover himself, but where the injury is more severe the advice of a doctor or trained medical 'orderly' (e.g. St John's Ambulance; physiotherapist) may be necessary in case the injury should require immediate treatment and/or a longer period of rest. The time must depend upon the advice given; and in the event of the time being excessive, the referee may order the match to be replayed the following day if this is possible. If play is resumed the same day, the match will carry on from the score at the time of the interruption; if a following day, the match begins again unless both players agree to carry on at the existing score. This rule applies to all interruptions in play, e.g. for light failure, dangerous floors, etc.

OBJECTION TO REFEREE

(a) **Before play.** The aim should be for the Officials (Referees and Markers) to be notified for matches to all concerned some hours (the previous day if possible) before play is scheduled. In this event the player may request a change not less than one hour before play; the Tournament Referee is not compelled to do so, but would be advised to make appropriate arrangements. Requests for a change within one hour of play or during the match should not be entertained unless made by both players.

(b) **During play.** The Tournament Director and/or Tournament Referee have the right to change the referee of a match if **both** players request it; the senior official should either himself, or appoint some other referee to, assess the match.

COLOURED CLOTHING

All players must adhere to Rule 25 – 'Players are required to wear white clothing. The Referee's decision thereon to be final'.

SERVICE

The service rule has been tidied up with, for instance, the addition of the wording allowing a player to 'drop' the ball and hit it, rather than apparently instructing him to throw it upwards.

There could be confusion about the word 'stand'. The intention is not for the server to have to be in a stationary position ('standing') necessarily.

Players may now appeal if they think the ball is out of court on the first service whether they play the ball or not. The appeal may be made either immediately or at the end of the rally if the ball is played.

KNOCK-UP

A new ball may be knocked up as may the ball in an interrupted match. Play will recommence at the direction of the Referee or prior mutual consent of the players.

No knocking-up between games is allowed without obtaining the opponent's permission. A game will be awarded if after due warning players persist in breaking this rule.

This rule has been introduced to prevent unseemly struggles for the ball at the end of a game when one player wants to warm it up and the other wants to cool it down.

Ball must remain on court and in view during the game interval.

MATCH BALL

The call of Match Ball is now made when Hand-in needs only to win the rally to win the match.